The Gauls

The Gauls

Celtic Antiquities
from
France

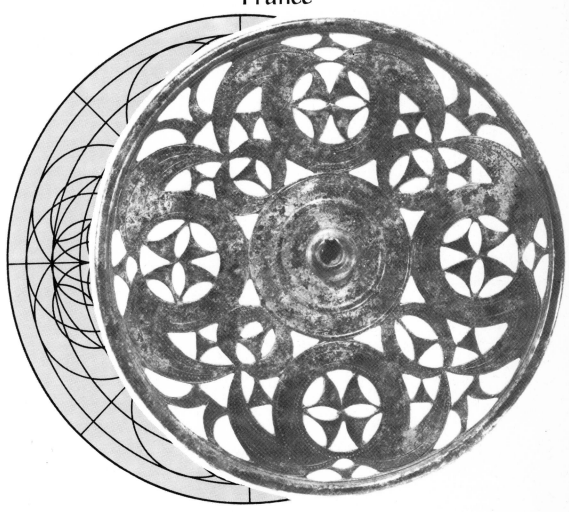

BMP Published for the
Trustees of the British Museum by
British Museum Publications Ltd

British Library Cataloguing in Publication Data

Stead, Ian
  The Gauls.
  1. France – Antiquities, Celtic – Exhibitions
  I. Title   II. British Museum
  III. Pengelly, Robert
  936.4'0074'02142   DC63
  ISBN 0-7141-2008-1

Published by British Museum Publications Ltd
46 Bloomsbury Street, London WC1B 3QQ
Designed by Harry Green
Set in Monotype Bembo by
S. H. Elder (Typesetters), Beverley, North Humberside
and printed in Great Britain by
Pindar Print, Scarborough and London

Abbreviations

CS	L. Morel, *La Champagne souterraine*, 1898.
ECA	P. Jacobsthal, *Early Celtic Art*, 1944.
PP	Sir Cyril Fox, *Pattern and Purpose: Early Celtic Art in Britain*, 1958.
Arras	I. M. Stead, *The Arras Culture*, 1979.
Champagne	D. Bretz-Mahler, *La civilisation de La Tène I en Champagne* (Gallia supplément xxiii), 1971.
Manuel	J. Déchelette, *Manuel d'Archéologie*, ii, 3me partie, *Second age du fer ou époque de La Tène*, 1914.

Measurements D: diameter H: height L: length W: width

Contents

Acknowledgements

The Trustees of the British Museum are grateful to the
French Government, through the good offices of
Messieurs Y. Mabin and D. Evesque, successive Cultural
Attachés at the Embassy in London, for suggesting this
exhibition and for financing the French contribution.
Most of the objects are from the Musée des antiquités
nationales, St Germain-en-Laye, and were selected by the
Conservateur-en-Chef, Monsieur R. Joffroy.

The following institutions and individuals have also
generously loaned exhibits: Musée Borély, Marseille
(nos 93, 94, 312 and 313); Musée St Remi, Reims (nos 223
and 233); Musée des Beaux-Arts, Besançon (no. 227);
Musée des Jacobins, Morlaix (no. 228); National Museum
of Wales (no. 255); Wisbech and Fenland Museum (no.
256); Cambridge University Museum of Archaeology and
Anthropology (no. 257); Museum of London, and the
Layton Memorial and Museum Trustees (no. 258); The
Duke of Northumberland (no. 261); Museums and Art
Galleries, Kingston-upon-Hull (no. 275); Yorkshire
Museum, York (nos 284 and 296); J. S. Dent (nos 285 and
297); British Museum (Natural History) (no. 286);
Somerset County Museum, Taunton (nos 299–303);
Castle Museum, Norwich (no. 308).

The photographs are reproduced by courtesy of the loan
institutions, the Commissioners of Public Works in Ireland, and Inge Kitlitschka.

The catalogue was written by I. M. Stead, with
contributions on the pottery by Valery Rigby and line
drawings by Robert Pengelly.

Preface

The culture of the Celts, whose distribution cannot be defined exactly, extended over the greater part of Central and Western Europe. On the Continent it lasted for about five centuries, comprising the whole of the second part of the Iron Age, the La Tène period, which is usually subdivided into La Tène I, (475–300 BC), La Tène II, (300–100 BC), and La Tène III, (100–52 BC).

La Tène I is well represented in the north-east of France, especially in Champagne, where the rich soils attracted a large population whose many burials, settlement remains and artefacts have led some writers to call this period 'Marnien' (after the Marne Département). There are several types of grave in Champagne: most are flat, with the skeleton extended on its back and accompanied by weapons or jewellery, whilst offerings of food were arranged in pottery vessels. Cremations, in small pits which contained cremated bones and grave-goods, are far less common. The richest and most interesting of the burials are the *tombes à char*, in which the deceased, chief or warrior, is inhumed on a two-wheeled war-chariot. It would have been a light vehicle of wood or wickerwork, but only the metal parts survive – the tyres, navehoops, phallera and horse-harness – so there is no basis for an accurate reconstruction of the vehicle itself. Although about 150 *tombes à char* can be listed, precise details are few because these rich graves often contained prestigious bronzes such as native helmets or imported Greco-Italian vessels, and thus fell victim to the greed of grave-robbers. It may be that these burials were covered by mounds, but this has yet to be proved. Certainly they had surrounding ditches, circular or quadrangular in plan, which were filled, like the central grave and the other 'flat' graves, with a dark earth whose origin is another mystery.

La Tène II is less well represented in France, doubtless because of migrations caused by pressure from the tribes known as 'Belgic'. Such migrations led to the invasion of North Italy and perhaps also Greece and Asia Minor, where the term *Galate* survives in place-names. Cremation becomes more common during La Tène II, and *tombes à char* are rare but more widely distributed. Grave-goods are mainly evolved from the earlier types, but more elegant forms of pottery were produced following the introduction of the potters' wheel.

La Tène III brought radical changes in all fields: lowland settlements were abandoned in favour of upland oppida; cremation became the general rule; there are new items of armament and dress which owe nothing to previous traditions; and the wheel-turned pottery includes innovations such as the so-called 'Roanne ware' with geometric or floral motifs painted on a white slip. La Tène III stops abruptly in 52 BC, the date of the battle of Alesia, which ended with the defeat of the most celebrated of all Gallic chiefs, Vercingetorix. That defeat left Gaul at the mercy of Caesar's armies, and marked the end not only of an epoque but of a culture. Although something of the old Celtic culture survived under the Roman occupation, as seen in works which owe nothing to romanisation, a new culture was created which transformed Gaul until the Barbarian invasions, the Gallo-Roman culture. This phenomenon is less obvious in the British Isles, and especially in the areas which escaped Roman influence, where a really original art-style developed, which is sometimes classified as La Tène IV.

R. JOFFROY
Conservateur-en-chef du Musée
des antiquités nationales

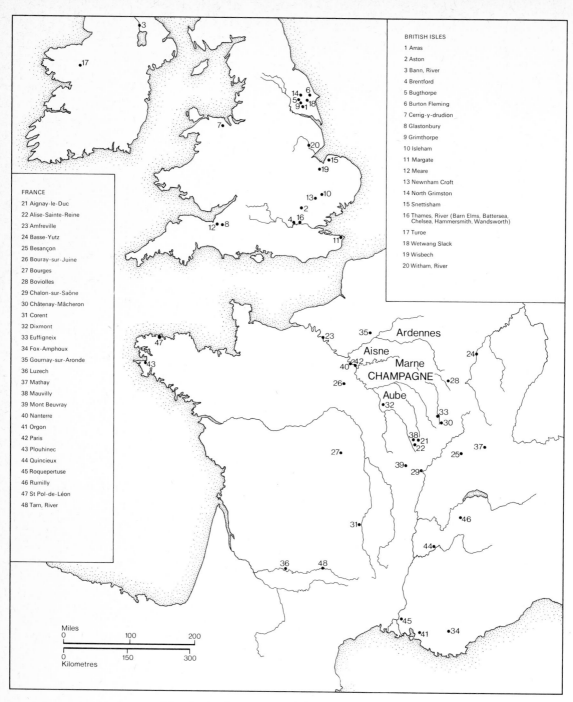

Miles
0   100   200

0   150   300
Kilometres

*Map showing the provenance of objects in the catalogue;
those from the Départements of Aisne, Ardennes, Aube and
Marne are not plotted individually.*

Introduction

This exhibition is based on a collection of Iron Age antiquities on loan from the Musée des antiquités nationales, enriched by eight outstanding pieces from other French museums, and some important French Iron Age antiquities from the British Museum collection. It assembles objects which have never before been seen together to illustrate the art of the Celts in France, and it introduces pieces of the British Iron Age to point some contrasts and similarities across the English Channel.

Κελτοι (Celtae), Galli and Galatae were alternative names used by classical writers for the same people, the Celts or Gauls. They were barbarians who lived to the north of the Mediterranean, from Britain in the west across to Hungary in the east, and even beyond, for the Galatians to whom St Paul wrote were in Asia Minor. In so far as they had any unity it was in their language, which was spoken but not generally written, and the Gauls themselves have left no account of their customs, beliefs and traditions. Instead, we know them vaguely from Greek and Roman writers, to whom they were strangers and often enemies, and from their often rich material remains. Because of the difficulties in correlation with historical records an independent classification of the artefacts is needed, and the scheme still used is basically that devised by the Swedish scholar Hans Hildebrand in 1872. The Iron Age of Celtic Europe is divided into an earlier (Hallstatt) and a later (La Tène) period, the division between the two falling in the middle of the fifth century BC. The La Tène period then continues until the Roman conquest - in France it is usually taken beyond Caesar's Gallic Wars to AD 1, and in southern Britain it is terminated by the Claudian conquest in AD 43. On the basis of the typology of artefacts the La Tène period is usually divided into three phases, to which conventional dates may be given: I (Early) 450–250 BC; II (Middle) 250–100 BC; III (Late) 100 BC to Roman times.

The Musée des antiquités nationales, in the château at St Germain-en-Laye only twenty-two kilometres from the centre of Paris, houses one of the finest collections of Celtic antiquities in the world. The present building, constructed by Francis I on the site of an earlier château, was used as a royal residence and became the last home of our own King James II, who died there in exile in 1718. After the French Revolution it was used as a prison and military barracks before being extensively restored to accommodate the national collection of antiquities. The museum was officially opened by the Emperor Napoléon III on 12 May 1867. Originally conceived as a Gallo-Roman museum, its horizons were soon widened to include national antiquities extending from the first appearance of Man to the time of Charlemagne. Napoléon's interest ensured that the museum got off to a good start, and he personally donated important collections. From the Second Empire to the First World War the museum expanded rapidly, with the acquisition of several extensive private collections. After the war the competition of provincial museums became more marked, but national treasures still found their way to St Germain-en-Laye.

There is a very strong bias towards Champagne in the national collection of Iron Age antiquities, and naturally this is reflected in the present exhibition. It is due in large part to the burial practices in north-east France, whereby all members of the community were accorded burial with grave-goods, which sometimes included collections of jewellery, weapons and domestic artefacts. Such burials are found particularly in the modern Département of Marne, and extend into Aube, Ardennes and Aisne. Although they have well-equipped graves, there is no real reason to suppose that the Gauls in Champagne were any richer than neighbours with simpler burial-rites. For instance, in north-west France and southern Britain at this time the dead were disposed of in an unknown way which has left no burials for comparison. Be that as it may, Champagne is of great importance because throughout the Iron Age its burials provide us with groups of associated, significant artefacts.

Attention was first drawn to Champagne by Napoléon III, who established an extensive military camp to the north of Châlons-sur-Marne in 1857. No doubt some burials were found by chance in the course of the construction of the camp, but certainly others were found deliberately when the emperor set his soldiers to dig. The imperial interest created a fashion, and Iron Age burials were sought all over Champagne. It has been estimated that between the 1860s and the outbreak of the First World War no fewer than 12,000 La Tène burials were discovered there. Unfortunately most of them were dug out with little regard to science, and very few grave-groups were kept intact. Some of the important collections went eventually to the Musée des antiquités nationales, and one – the Morel collection – was acquired by the British Museum. Many of the collections which remained locally were destroyed when Champagne became a world battleground twice within thirty years.

The Great Collectors

Napoléon III

Charles Louis Napoléon Bonaparte (1808–73) (pl. 1) was not only the founder of the Musée des antiquités nationales, but also the instigator of excavations whose discoveries enriched its collections. The son of Louis Bonaparte, King of Holland, and the nephew of the great Napoléon, Louis Napoléon spent his early life in exile, returning to France in 1848 to progress rapidly via the presidency of the Second Republic and a *coup d'état* to become the Emperor Napoléon III. He lost his throne in the débâcle of the Franco-Prussian War, at Sedan in 1870, and died shortly afterwards in exile in England.

A scholar as well as a politician, he planned a biography of Charlemagne while in prison at Ham, near St Quentin, but research facilities proved too limited. The Tuilerie Palace provided a more congenial centre for study, and Napoléon's second biographical attempt was much more successful. Two out of three projected volumes of his *Histoire de Jules César* were published in 1865 and 1866. With a view to setting his Caesarian researches on a sound basis Napoléon organised several important excavations, and commissioned plans, relief models, and reconstructions of Roman weapons. The Musée des antiquités nationales was devised in part to house this collection.

Every year, in the late summer, Napoléon III visited the Camp de Châlons for a fortnight to take part in the manoeuvres, and it was there that he observed, and ordered the excavation of, La Tène burials. He acquired other antiquities by gift and purchase from collectors and excavators in the area. The Champenois who dealt with the emperor were mainly peasants, and one of the most successful, Jean-Babtiste Counhaye, was a travelling grocer. But they were not scholars, and they did not record their excavating activities. We know as little about the personalities and opinions of these collectors as we do about their excavations, but there must have been many stories to be told about them. Indeed, the fate of Denis Machet, of St Etienne-au-Temple, said to have been drowned by a jealous rival, suggests that it might have been a field worthy of Zola's attention.

Nos 1–22 were acquired by Napoléon III. The majority are from St Etienne-au-Temple, where there were at least four La Tène cemeteries, and were formerly in the Machet Collection.

1 Biconical carinated dish, La Tène I
St Etienne-au-Temple (Marne). Handmade. H 48mm.
M.A.N. 15396.

2 Tripartite carinated beaker, La Tène I
St Etienne-au-Temple (Marne). Handmade. H 108mm.
M.A.N. 5024.

3 Tripartite carinated beaker, La Tène I
Camp de Châlons (Marne). Handmade. H 215mm.
M.A.N. 77071.

4 Tripartite carinated jar, La Tène I
St Etienne-au-Temple (Marne). Handmade. H 115mm.
M.A.N. 13881.

5 Tulip-shaped beaker, La Tène I
St Etienne-au-Temple (Marne). Handmade. H 140mm.
M.A.N. 12879.

6 Tulip-shaped beaker, La Tène I
St Etienne-au-Temple (Marne). Handmade. H 103mm.
M.A.N. 12877.

7 Tulip-shaped jar, La Tène I
St Etienne-au-Temple (Marne). Handmade. H 280mm.
M.A.N. 12894.

8 Shouldered jar, La Tène I
St Etienne-au-Temple (Marne). Handmade. H 260mm.
M.A.N. 13881.

9 Ovoid jar, La Tène I
St Etienne-au-Temple (Marne). Handmade. H 236mm.
M.A.N. 15389.

10 Bent iron sword in an iron scabbard, La Tène I
St Etienne-au-Temple (Marne). L (present state)
340mm, (when straight) 575mm. M.A.N. 13509.

11 Bent iron sword, La Tène I
St Etienne-au-Temple (Marne). L (present state
265mm, (when straight) 705mm. M.A.N. 13508.

12 Iron sword in iron scabbard, La Tène I
St Etienne-au-Temple (Marne). L 685mm.
M.A.N. 13520a. *Champagne* pl. 88, no.4.

13 Iron sword in iron scabbard, La Tène II
St Etienne-au-Temple (Marne). L 660mm. M.A.N. 13502b.

14 Iron shield-boss, La Tène II
St Etienne-au-Temple (Marne). L 207mm.
M.A.N. 13513.

15 Bronze torque, La Tène I
St Etienne-au-Temple (Marne). D 185mm.
M.A.N. 12739.

16 Two bronze bracelets, La Tène I
Départment Marne. D 60, 62mm. M.A.N. 12972 and 3.

17 Bronze bracelet, La Tène I or II
St Rémy-sur-Bussy (Marne). D 57mm. M.A.N. 4797.

18 Bronze bracelet, La Tène I/II
St Rémy-sur-Bussy (Marne). D 66mm. M.A.N. 4794.

19 Shale bracelet, La Tène I
St Etienne-au-Temple (Marne). D 80mm. M.A.N. 3096.

20 Bead necklace, La Tène I
L'Epine (Marne). 48 blue glass (D 4mm) and 10 amber
(D c. 12mm) beads. M.A.N. 16053.

21 Glass bracelet, La Tène III
La Croix-en-Champagne (Marne). D 85mm.
M.A.N. 13140.

22 Glass bead, La Tène I
St Etienne-au-Temple (Marne). D 26mm.
M.A.N. 12717.

Frédéric Moreau

Frédéric Moreau (1798–1898) (pl. 1) came late to
archaeology, in his mid-seventies, but that still left
plenty of time for one who lived to see his hundredth
birthday. He started his excavations in 1873, after his
retirement, by excavating a 'dolmen' near the Caranda
Mill, Cierges, Aisne, not far from the source of the
River Ourcq. The dolmen was surrounded by a vast
cemetery – Iron Age, Roman and Merovingian – and
Moreau's excavations there in 1874 and 1875 provided the
nucleus of his collection. He carried out further excavations annually until 1893, centred on Fère-en-Tardenois
and extending from the Aisne to the Marne. His collection
was available for study at his home, 98 rue de la Victoire,
Fère-en-Tardenois, and in 1878 it was shown at the Paris
International Exhibition. In 1877 Moreau published the
first part of an illustrated volume known as the *Album
Caranda*, and subsequent parts were issued up to 1898.
This work was never paginated and the numbering of the
plates is confusing, and so it is a bibliographical nightmare
to which later scholars have had to publish a collation and
guide. In his will Moreau left his collection to the national
museums, on condition that 20,000 francs were paid
towards the restoration of the belfry in his home town.

The collection entered St Germain-en-Laye in 1899 and
was displayed in a room named after Moreau.

It is instructive to compare the selection of pottery
from the Moreau collection with the exhibits from the
Morel and Napoléon III collections excavated further to
the east and south. Comparison of similar forms, nos 30
with 184 and 27 with 171, highlights differences of
detail and decoration. Although selection may have
exaggerated the differences, there are no really close
parallels to nos 24, 30 and 34 in the whole of the Morel
collection which numbers some 260 Iron Age pots. The
contrast seems to be regional rather than chronological.

23 Conical beaker, La Tène I
Ciry-Salsogne (Aisne). Handmade. H 168mm.
M.A.N. 42326.

24 Biconical carinated dish, La Tène I
Ciry-Salsogne (Aisne). Handmade. H 80mm.
M.A.N. 42617.

25 Biconical carinated goblet, La Tène I
Ciry-Salsogne (Aisne). Handmade. H 129mm.
M.A.N. 42519.

26 Tripartite carinated beaker, La Tène I
Chassemy (Aisne). Handmade. H 210mm.
M.A.N. 17878.

27 Biconical carinated jar, La Tène I
Chassemy (Aisne). Handmade. H 122mm.
M.A.N. 42515.

28 Bell-shaped goblet, La Tène I
Ciry-Salsogne (Aisne). Handmade. H 127mm.
M.A.N. 42440.

29 Ovoid beaker, La Tène I
Ciry-Salsogne (Aisne). Handmade. H 230mm.
M.A.N. 42446.

30 Ovoid goblet, La Tène I
Ciry-Salsogne (Aisne). Handmade. H 125mm.
M.A.N. 424. (PLATE 2)

31 Tulip-shaped beaker, La Tène I
Ciry-Salsogne (Aisne). Handmade. H 330mm.
M.A.N. 42430.

32 Tulip-shaped beaker, La Tène I
Ciry-Salsogne (Aisne). Handmade. H 347mm.
M.A.N. 42427.

33 Tulip-shaped beaker, La Tène I
Ciry-Salsogne (Aisne). Handmade. H 228mm.
M.A.N. 42439.

34 Tripartite carinated beaker, La Tène II
Ciry-Salsogne (Aisne). Handmade. H 200mm.
M.A.N. 42470.

35 Bronze jewellery, La Tène I
Chouy (Aisne). Torque (D 177mm) and pair of
bracelets (D 68mm). M.A.N. 39242, 37616.

36 Bronze jewellery, La Tène I
Martroy de Lime (Aisne). Torque (D 218mm), bracelet
(D 75mm), long pendant (L 90mm), two pendant-rings
(D 66mm), two rings (D 21, 24mm). M.A.N. 39241,
39122, 39273, 39196, 38252.

Léon Morel

Léon Morel (1828–1909) (pl. 1) first interested himself in
archaeology when he was a young tax-collector at
Somsois, near Vitry-le-François, in 1863. A La Tène
cemetery had been discovered in the course of roadworks,
and Morel completed its excavation and produced a
commendable report. He was subsequently moved to
two other posts in Champagne, near Sezanne and
Châlons-sur-Marne, before promotion took him south to
Provence in 1879. Already in 1874 Morel claimed to have
explored more than fifteen cemeteries in Champagne. He
concluded his career by returning to Vitry-le-François
in 1888, and then retired to live at Reims.

Morel published papers and gave lectures on his
archaeological finds throughout his working life, but
only his early excavations were recorded in adequate
detail. His important contribution to archaeological
literature was *La Champagne souterraine* (1898), a collection
of excavation reports including several reprinted from
earlier versions in learned journals. The accompanying
Album consisted of thirty-six plates of lithographs and
appeared in six parts between 1875 and 1879.

At first Morel was closely involved with work in the
field, but as time went on he relied increasingly on the
work of others, and much of his collection was purchased
from other excavators or dealers. The Morel collection
was displayed at the international exhibitions which were
such a feature of Paris at the end of the nineteenth
century (the Trocadero, 1878; Champ de Mars, 1889;
Petit Palais, 1900), and it was universally acknowledged
as the finest collection of French antiquities outside
St Germain-en-Laye. In the 1890s Morel's collection was
on display at his home, 3 rue de Sedan, Reims, and at the
turn of the century he decided to sell. It was offered to the
Musée des antiquités nationales, but was considered too
expensive because much of it duplicated material already
in the museum. The British Museum then took its
opportunity, and purchased a major collection which has
proved an invaluable source of comparative material, an
extensive field for study, and a stimulus for research. The
collection is now housed in four Departments (Coins &
Medals, Greek & Roman, Medieval & Later, and
Prehistoric & Romano-British Antiquities), and the Iron
Age items alone amount to 1631 pieces.

37 Conical beaker, La Tène I
Courtisols (Marne). Handmade. H 88mm.
B.M. ML.2676.

38 Biconical carinated bowl and jar, La Tène I
Bergères-lès-Vertus (Marne). Handmade. H 52, 140mm.
B.M. ML.2657. (PLATE 15)

39 Tripartite carinated jar, La Tène I
St Rémy-sur-Bussy (Marne). Handmade. H 132mm.
B.M. ML.2703. (PLATE 15)

40 Tripartite carinated jar, La Tène I
Loisy-en-Brie (Marne). Handmade. H 188mm.
B.M. ML.2721.

41 Tulip-shaped bowl, La Tène I
Courtisols (Marne). Handmade. H 104mm.
B.M. ML.2679.

42 Necked and shouldered flask, La Tène I
Suippes (Marne). Handmade. H 156mm.
B.M. ML.2961.

**43 Shouldered jar with trumpet-shaped
pedestalled base,** La Tène I/II
St Rémy-sur-Bussy (Marne). Wheelmade. H 260mm.
B.M. ML.2732. (PLATE 17)

**44 Shouldered jar with trumpet-shaped
pedestalled base,** La Tène I
Prosnes (Marne). Wheelmade. H 272mm. B.M. ML.2666.
(PLATE 39)

45 Iron sword in the remains of an iron scabbard,
La Tène I
Marson (Marne). L 657mm. B.M. ML.1516. *CS* pl. 2,
fig. 10.

46 Iron knife, La Tène I
Prosnes (Marne). L 315mm. B.M. ML.1595. *CS* pl. 24,
fig. 1. (PLATE 2)

47 Iron spear-head, La Tène I
Marson (Marne). L 191mm. B.M. ML.1509. *CS* pl. 2,
fig. 7.

48 Iron spear-head, La Tène I
Courtisols (Marne). L 459mm. B.M. ML.1637.
CS pl. 29, fig. 1.

49 Bronze torque, La Tène I
Département Marne. D 156mm. B.M. ML.1717.
CS pl. 38, fig. 6.

50 Bronze torque, La Tène I
Courtisols (Marne). D 210mm. B.M. ML.1654.
CS pl. 29, fig. 22.

51 Bronze torque, La Tène I
Bussy-le-Château (Marne). D 133mm. B.M. ML.1683.
CS pl. 34, fig. 18.

52 Bronze torque, La Tène I
St Rémy-sur-Bussy (Marne). D 152mm. B.M. ML.1816.

53 Bronze bracelet, La Tène I
'Charvais', Heiltz-l'Evêque (Marne). D 63mm.
B.M. ML.1858.

54 Bronze bracelet, La Tène I
Provenance unknown (Champagne). D 65mm.
B.M. ML.1836.

55 Bronze bracelet, La Tène I
Provenance unknown (Champagne). D 61mm.
B.M. ML.1834.

56 Bronze brooch, La Tène I
Somme-Bionne (Marne). L 52mm. B.M. ML.1429.
CS pl. 14, fig. 5.

57 Bronze brooch, La Tène I
Ognes (Marne). L 69mm. B.M. ML.1826.

Marquis de Baye

Amour Auguste Louis Joseph Berthelot (1853–1931)
(pl. 1), Baron, then Marquis, de Baye had his ancestral
home the château at Baye, south of Epernay, on the edge
of the Marais de St Gond – one of the richest archaeological areas in Champagne. As a young man the Baron de
Baye started to explore sites of all periods in the area,
from Neolithic to Merovingian, including a number of
important Iron Age cemeteries. In particular, he established himself as an authority on Merovingian and other
contemporary jewellery. The Baron's other academic
love was for the people and culture of Russia, where he
spent much time on scientific missions. The outbreak of
the First World War found him in Petrograd, and he was
still in Russia three years later when the Revolution led
to his imprisonment. Meanwhile the Château de Baye
had been sacked, and his collections and papers destroyed
in the war in Champagne. Fortunately some time
previously, in 1909, the Baron had donated important
archaeological collections to the Musée des antiquités
nationales, where they were grouped in one room which
was given his name. The de Baye collection has recently
been studied by A. Thenot, whose thesis awaits publication.

58 Biconical carinated jar, La Tène I
Charmont (Marne). Handmade. H 148mm.
M.A.N. 67845.

59 Iron spear-head with bent point, La Tène I
Charmont (Marne). L (when straight) 400mm.
M.A.N. 67808.

60 Iron spear-head, La Tène I
Charmont (Marne). L 338mm. M.A.N. 67801.

61 Iron dagger with bone hilt, La Tène I
Bussy-le-Château (Marne). L 290mm. M.A.N. 67906.
Champagne 92, pl. 85, no. 3. (PLATE 2)

62 Bronze jewellery, La Tène I
Tilloy (Marne). Torque (D 157mm), a pair of bracelets
(D 68mm), and a large ring (D 49mm). M.A.N. 67828.
Champagne pl. 33, no. 4 (torque), and pl. 65, no. 2
(bracelet).

63 Bronze bracelet, La Tène I/II
Somme-Suippes (Marne). D 66mm. M.A.N. 67948.

64 Bronze jewellery, La Tène I
Somme-Suippes (Marne). Pair of bracelets (D 65mm)
and brooch (L 66mm). M.A.N. 67955.

65 Bronze jewellery, La Tène I
Tilloy (Marne). Torque (D 200mm), pair of bracelets
(D 70mm). M.A.N. 67927. *Champagne* pl. 34, no. 2
(torque), and pl. 65, no. 1 (bracelet).

66 Bronze and iron jewellery, La Tène I
Somme-Suippes (Marne). Bronze torque (D 142mm),
bronze bracelet (D 67mm), iron bracelet (D 87mm).
M.A.N. 67947.

67 Bronze torque with three projecting ornaments,
La Tène I
Flavigny (Marne). D 170mm. M.A.N. 67873. J. de
Baye, 'Sépultures gauloises de Flavigny', *Rev. Arch.*
ii (1877), 40–6, pl. xiv, no. 2. (PLATE 2)

68 Bronze bracelet, La Tène I
Somme-Suippes (Marne). D 60mm. M.A.N. 67945.
Associated with the torque, no. 156.

Burials in Champagne

The overall sequence of burials in Champagne is clearly established, and the changing pattern of funerary customs provides the archaeologist with a useful chronological framework. Iron came into use in the first half of the first millennium BC when the burial practice was cremation, but in the fifth century BC inhumation became fashionable, often with rich collections of grave-goods. The second century saw a reversion to cremation, still with grave-goods, and this rite continued into Roman times. The nineteenth-century excavators were particularly adept at discovering inhumations, partly because the graves were often filled with distinctive dark earth ('*terre noire*') which contrasted with the surrounding chalky soil. Hence their collections, and this exhibition, are dominated by grave-goods of the La Tène I period and the earlier part of La Tène II, whereas the pottery and other finds from La Tène III cremations are hardly represented at all.

Somme-Bionne

One of the richest La Tène burials from Champagne was found in 1873 in a locality known, significantly, as 'L'Homme Mort' in the commune of Somme-Bionne, thirty kilometres north-east of Châlons-sur-Marne. It was discovered by the younger Hanusse – father and son lived at La Croix-en-Champagne, and between them excavated many graves (by 1885 it was said that they had excavated 1050 La Tène burials). Léon Morel soon acquired the finds, and his account of the discovery implies that he was personally involved in the excavation of the harness-trench, which could have been overlooked in an initial excavation. Subsequently Morel was associated with Hanusse in the excavation of other graves in the cemetery. Because of the way in which this burial was discovered some scholars have alleged that it is not a true grave-group, but was deliberately made up for sale to Morel. This is certainly a possibility, but there seems no real reason to distrust it any more than the other grave-groups recovered under similar circumstances about that time.

The body had been buried along with the remains of a two-wheeled vehicle, which seems likely to have been intact when it was placed in the large grave (no. 69). The grave was rectangular, 2.85m by 1.80m, and 1.15m deep; below its floor two separate cuttings had been excavated to accommodate the wheels, while at the front a narrow trench to take the pole terminated in a cross-trench which held pieces of harness. The entire grave was at the centre of a circular area defined by a ditch 16m diameter and 1m deep, and it seems very likely that this marked the outline of a barrow.

The skeleton was extended, and had a long sword in a bronze scabbard on its right side and three iron rods of unknown function on its left. There was an iron knife over the left forearm and the remains of a belt around the waist. Beyond the feet was a native pot, a Greek cup, a bronze Etruscan flagon and a piece of openwork gold which might well have ornamented a drinking horn. In the harness trench were two horse-bits, two phalera and openwork bronzes which were once mounted on leather straps. The Greek cup was made about 420 BC, which gives the earliest possible date for the grave.

69 Contents of a cart-burial, La Tène I
Somme-Bionne (Marne). B.M. ML.1338–1406, 2713.
CS 23–80, pls. 7–12. (PLATE 3)

Cart-burials

At least 140 burials in Champagne had the remains of carts with them, and most seem to follow the pattern of Somme-Bionne. All the vehicles had been intact with upright wheels a standard 1.3m apart, and separate wheel-holes were a regular feature. Some graves lacked the pole-trench and harness-trench, and some instead had the harness arranged on a wide shelf towards the front (e.g. Somme-Tourbe, 'La Gorge-Meillet'). Not all the occupants of the carts were warriors, and indeed some were certainly women. This raises the problem of the function of the vehicle, often identified as a war-chariot, and suggests that for this last journey it was simply a hearse. On the other hand the vehicles usually show some sign of wear, and must have had an everyday function as well, perhaps as a multi-purpose vehicle: 'For their journeys and in battle they use two-horse chariots' (Diodorus Siculus v. 29. 1).

The principle remains of the vehicles are iron tyres which bound wooden wheels (Fig. 1). The wooden rim of the wheel – the felloe – was made from a single length of wood whose terminals overlapped in a scarf joint and were secured by an iron clamp (no. 71). The hubs, or naves, were bound with iron bands (no. 72) on either

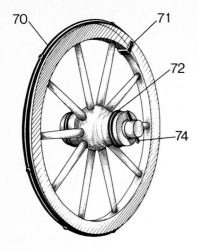

Fig. 1 Reconstruction of a Gallic wheel.

side of the spokes, and the wheel was held on the axle by a linch-pin (nos 74–6). Little or nothing survives from the body of the vehicle, which would have been made entirely of wood. Iron ring-ended fittings, often linked (nos 77–78), are quite regularly found between the two wheels, but their function is unknown. Of the pole, the terminal is sometimes found (no. 229), but normally it must have been made of wood. The cart was drawn by two horses, whose bits are often found (nos 79–80), and they were linked by a yoke, which occasionally had decorative metal plates (no. 231).

70 Two iron cart-tyres, La Tène I
Provenance unknown (Champagne). D 870mm.
M.A.N. 61516.

71 Iron felloe-clamp, La Tène I
Somme-Bionne (Marne). L 78mm. B.M. ML.1386.
CS pl. 12, fig. 4.

72 Two iron nave-hoops, La Tène I
Provenance unknown (Champagne). D 155mm.
M.A.N. 12919.

73 Two iron discs to fit the ends of naves,
La Tène I
Provenance unknown (Champagne). D 120mm.
M.A.N. 13360.

74 Iron linch-pin, La Tène I
St Etienne-au-Temple (Marne). L 130mm.
M.A.N. 13382.

75 Iron linch-pin, La Tène I
Provenance unknown (Champagne). L 140mm.
M.A.N. 20274.

76 Iron linch-pin, La Tène II
'Nanterre' = Colombes (Hauts-de-Seine). The bronze head has a red glass inlay. L 135mm. M.A.N. 36139.
H. Hubert, 'Sépulture à char de Nanterre', *Congrès int. d'anthrop. et d'arch. préhist.* 12 (1900) 410–17, fig. 11;
Manuel fig. 502, no. 7.

77 Linked iron rods, La Tène I
Provenance unknown (Champagne). L 155, 85mm.
M.A.N. 13378.

78 Linked iron rods, La Tène I
Provenance unknown (Champagne).
L 230, 95mm. M.A.N. 27877.

79 Iron horse-bit, La Tène I
Vicinity of the Camp de Châlons (Marne). L 298mm.
M.A.N. 16023. (PLATE 4)

80 Iron horse-bit, La Tène I
Provenance unknown (Champagne). L 283mm.
B.M. ML.2567.

Weapons

'The whole race . . . is madly fond of war, high-spirited and quick to battle' (Strabo IV.4.2), and warriors were often laid to rest with their full complement of weapons. Spears are most frequently found, often two or three in a grave. The wooden shafts have long since perished, so the remains comprise the iron heads and sometimes the pointed iron butts from the opposite end (no. 81). Daggers and swords are found more rarely, and there is never more than the one to a grave. The fashionable weapon in Late Hallstatt times was a short dagger, often kept in a bronze sheath, but in the fifth century it was replaced by the much longer iron sword, usually in an iron scabbard (no. 86). Sometimes swords (no. 87), and occasionally also daggers (no. 271), were deliberately bent before being buried. One can only guess about the significance of this ritual, which would have left the warrior with a useless weapon for any battles in the after-life, but inevitably it recalls a famous passage in Polybius. Describing the battles of the Gauls in Italy in the middle of the third century BC, Polybius (II.33) comments on the weakness of their swords, which 'could only give one downward thrust with any effect, but that after this the edges got so turned, and the blade so bent, that unless they had time to straighten them with their foot against the ground, they could not deliver a second blow'. However, this historical account scarcely tallies with recent scientific examinations of La Tène swords, which show that some sword-smiths took pains to produce tough weapons. Salomon Reinach suggested that archaeological evidence could have influenced Polybius, for either directly or indirectly he could have come across bent swords in burials of the Gauls in northern Italy, and accepting the time-honoured misconception linking cemeteries with battlefields he could have misinterpreted these ritually bent weapons for the swords of those killed by the Romans.

Metal helmets are but rarely found in graves and the usual La Tène I type, represented here by examples from Somme-Tourbe (no. 89) and Berru (no. 222), was elegantly shaped. Whether or not it would have been effective in battle is another matter, and the later form which fits the head closely seems more practical (no. 90). Early historians refer to quite elaborate Gaulish helmets: 'on their heads they wear bronze helmets which possess large projecting figures lending the appearance of enormous stature to the wearer; in some cases horns form one piece with the helmet, while in other cases it is relief figures of the foreparts of birds or quadrupeds' (Diodorus Siculus v.30.2). But it is difficult to correlate this account with surviving artefacts from France, although there is a British horned helmet from the River Thames and a Rumanian helmet surmounted by a magnificent bird. Horned helmets are also depicted in stone and bronze, but most classical representations of Gallic warriors show them bare-headed (nos 91 and 92). Doubtless leather helmets were also worn: they are depicted on stone sculptures (no. 93) and traces of one were noted at Cuperly along with nos 235 and 238, but usually leather stands little chance of preservation in graves.

'They wear a striking kind of clothing – tunics dyed and stained in various colours, and trousers, which they call by the name of *bracae*' (Diodorus Siculus v.30.1). The small figurine of a Gaulish prisoner, hands tied behind his back, gives an excellent picture of chequered trousers (no. 92). Warriors in battle seem normally to have worn trousers, with or without cloaks (no. 91). Polybius describes the warriors of the Gallic tribes at the Battle of Telamon (225 BC): 'the Insubres and Boii were clothed in their breeches and light cloaks; but the Gaesatae from vanity and bravado threw these garments away, and fell in front of the army naked, with nothing but their arms'. Naked warriors impressed other early historians – 'some have iron breast-plates of chain-mail while others fight naked, and for them the breast-plate given by Nature suffices' (Diodorus Siculus v.29.3) – and are known from classical representations as well. Diodorus Siculus referred to mail-shirts, and this is supported by occasional finds from Celtic contexts, whilst sculptures from the south of France show both mail-shirts and leather cuirasses (no. 94).

Shields were made mainly, sometimes entirely, of organic materials which have not survived in the Champagne graves. Their shapes are known from contemporary examples found in more favourable conditions, usually waterlogged, and from classical representations in stone. The graves have produced a few metal fittings, although in La Tène I this normally amounted to no more than an iron handle (nos 95 and 96) and only rarely was metal used on the front (no. 277). At the end of La Tène I and early in La Tène II the 'twinned' boss is found, with a pair of rectangular iron plates mounted on either side of the central spine (no. 97). This was superceded by the band-shaped iron umbo, which crossed the boss and had broad side-plates attached to the main body of the shield (no. 98). Circular shield-bosses are occasionally found in La Tène III contexts (no. 99).

Other artefacts discovered with warriors include large knives (nos 46 and 100), which are sometimes alongside the remains of pigs in the graves. These excellent multi-purpose knives could have served the cook, hunter and, if need be, the warrior too. Two other objects sometimes found in men's graves, occasionally together, are a pair of iron shears (no. 101) and a razor (no. 102) – essential items for warriors who took a pride in their appearance: 'some shave off the beard, while others cultivate a short beard; the nobles shave the cheeks but let the moustache grow freely so that it covers the mouth' (Diodorus Siculus v.28.3).

81 Four iron spear-heads and four iron spear-butts, La Tène I
La Croix-en-Champagne (Marne). L (spear-heads) 280, 250, 330, 240mm, (spear-butts) 97, 87, 87, 70mm.
M.A.N. 67820.

82 Large iron spear-head, La Tène II
Fère-Champenoise (Marne). Decorated with perforations. L 616mm. M.A.N. 1675 BL.
A Brisson, 'Le cimetière gaulois de "La Fin d'Ecury' commune de Fère-Champenoise (Marne)', *Bull. Soc. Arch. Champenoise* (1935) 72–9, fig. 4. (PLATE 4)

83 Short iron sword in bronze and iron scabbard, La Tène I
Charmont (Marne). L 439mm. M.A.N. 67808/8.
Champagne pl. 86, no. 7.

84 Short iron sword in a bronze and iron scabbard, La Tène I
St Jean-sur-Tourbe (Marne). L 450mm. M.A.N. 33282.
Champagne pl. 86, no. 3.

85 Iron sword, La Tène I
Auberive (Marne). L 645mm. M.A.N. 8123.

86 Iron sword in the remains of an iron scabbard, La Tène II
Corroy (Marne). L 960mm. B.M. ML.2937. R. A. Smith, *A guide to the antiquities of the Early Iron Age* (British Museum) (1925) pl. ix, no. 5 (PLATE 5)

87 Bent iron sword, La Tène I
Rumilly (Haute-Savoie). L (when straight) 590mm.
M.A.N. 13854.

88 Iron chain for attaching a sword-scabbard,
La Tène II
Provenance unknown (Champagne). L (when straight)
470, 129mm. B.M. ML.2570 and 2573. (PLATE 5)

89 Bronze helmet, La Tène I
'La Gorge-Meillet', Somme-Tourbe (Marne). H 380mm.
M.A.N. 24917. E. Fourdrignier, *Double sépulture
gauloise de la Gorge-Meillet, territoire de Somme-Tourbe
(Marne)* (1878) pl. vii; *Manuel* fig. 490, no. 4; *ECA*
no. 135. (PLATE 5)

90 Bronze helmet, La Tène III
Coolus (Marne). H 129mm. B.M. ML.1734. L. Morel,
note in *Bull. Soc. Nat. Antiquaires France* (1875) 113–14;
CS 168–72, pl. 39, fig. 2; H. Russell Robinson, *The
Armour of Imperial Rome* (1975) 26, fig. 35, pl. 37.
(PLATE 6)

91 Bronze figurine of a Gaulish warrior, Roman
Imperial
Provenance unknown. H 64mm. B.M. (Greek &
Roman Antiquities) 78.10–19.54. H. B.Walters,
*Catalogue of the Bronzes, Greek Roman and Etruscan . . .
British Museum* (1899) no. 817. (PLATE 6)

92 Bronze figurine of a Gaulish prisoner,
Roman Imperial
Provenance unknown. H 72mm. B.M. (Greek &
Roman Antiquities) 59.11–26.1. Walters, *op. cit.,*
no. 818. (PLATE 6)

**93 Limestone head of a man wearing a leather
helmet,** La Tène III
Orgon (Bouches-du-Rhône). H 260mm. Musée
Borély, Marseille. E. Esperandieu, *Recueil général des
bas-reliefs, statues et bustes de la Gaule romaine,* ix (1925)
100–101, no. 6701; F. Benoit, *L'art primitif
méditerranéen de la vallée du Rhône* (1955) pl. xli, no. 1.
(PLATE 7)

**94 Limestone torso of a man wearing what is
probably a leather cuirasse,** La Tène III
Fox-Amphoux (Var). Part of a shield is visible on one
side. H 420mm. Musée Borély, Marseille. Benoit,
op. cit., pl. xl, nos 1 and 2. (PLATE 8)

95 Iron handle of a shield, La Tène I
St Etienne-au-Temple (Marne). L 190mm.
M.A.N. 13515.

96 Iron handle of a shield, La Tène I
Somme-Bionne (Marne). L 154mm.
B.M. ML.1495.

97 Shield-boss composed of two iron plaques,
La Tène I/II
Somme-Suippes (Marne). L 80mm. M.A.N. 64466.
For the type, the twinned (*zweischalig*) shield-boss,
see W. Krämer, 'Zur Zeitstellung der hölzernen
Schilde des Hirschsprungfundes', *Prähist. Zeitschr.* 34–5
(1949–50) 354–60 (listed p. 357, note 18); and other
French examples, J. M. de Navarro *The finds from the
site of La Tène, i, Scabbards and the swords found in them*
(1972) 74, note 1.

98 Iron shield-boss mounted on a replica shield,
La Tène II
Département Marne. W 215mm. B.M. ML.2873.
(PLATE 9)

99 Circular iron shield-boss, La Tène III
Clamanges (Marne). Found with the brooch, no. 148.
D 165mm. M.A.N. 1654 BL. (PLATE 13)

100 Large iron knife, La Tène I
La Croix-en-Champagne (Marne). L 350mm.
M.A.N. 67820.

101 Pair of iron shears, La Tène I
Provenance unknown (Champagne). L 203mm.
B.M. ML.2565. (PLATE 9)

102 Iron razor, La Tène III
Asfeld (Ardennes). L 70mm. B.M. ML.2887. *Bull.
Arch.* (1894) xci and xcviii. (PLATE 9)

Jewellery

In Champagne it was the practice to bury a woman with
the jewellery she wore in everyday life, and the changing
fashion is an invaluable aid to chronology. Some well-
authenticated complete sets of jewellery survive, but
many of the items now available for study are devoid of
associations. This is due in part to the attitude of the
nineteenth-century collectors, who were more interested
in the objects than in their context. But even when a
grave was carefully excavated and fully recorded, it is
not always certain that the complete range of jewellery
was recovered. A large number of graves had been
disturbed and both grave-goods and bones removed or
displaced at some time before the collectors excavated
them.

Where complete sets of jewellery survive (nos 103–112)
it can be shown that women in Early La Tène times in
Champagne often wore a torque (neck-ring) and two
bracelets, one on each arm. In La Tène II torques are much
less common, and it was more usual to wear a single
bracelet than a pair. The tiny bronze figurine (no. 113)
is one of the few representations of a Gallic woman to
survive from antiquity: she wears a torque and bracelets,
and apparently little else, but although depicting a La

Tène I fashion the figurine is stylistically of the Roman Imperial period.

Apart from the jewellery that they wore, we know very little about Gallic women. Classical writers are not informative, for unfortunately the relevant passage in the lost *History* of Posidonius was not subsequently quoted. An odd line may have survived in Diodorus Siculus (v.32.2) where it is recorded that the women are 'not only equal to their husbands in stature, but they rival them in strength as well'. Ammianus Marcellinus (xv.12.1) elaborates on this, and was obviously terrified of Gallic women: 'a whole band of foreigners would be unable to cope with a single Gaul, if he called his wife to his aid, who is usually very strong and with blue eyes; especially when swelling her neck, gnashing her teeth and brandishing her sallow arms of huge proportions, she begins to strike blows mingled with kicks, as if they had been so many bolts sent from the string of a catapult'. In Britain in the middle of the first century AD two women wielded political power, Queens Cartimandua of the Brigantes and Boudicca of the Iceni, whilst on the Continent women as well as men were buried in rich graves.

The following sets of jewellery were worn by Gallic ladies in Champagne from the fifth to the third centuries BC:

103 Group of jewellery, La Tène I
Bussy-le-Château (Marne). Two bronze torques (D 215, 196mm), four bronze bracelets (D 72, 70, 70, 65mm), two glass bracelets (D 61, 63mm), two bronze rings (D 23, 27mm), bronze pendant (L 55mm), bronze belt-hook (L 65mm), pair of bronze brooches (L 65mm) linked by a bronze chain (L 310mm), three more bronze brooches (L 57, 35, 46mm). Two pots found in the grave are not included in this exhibition. M.A.N. 67883.
Despite the large number of objects in this grave, scholars who have studied it are satisfied that there was only the one inhumation – certainly skeletons with two torques have been excavated in modern times (at Villeneuve-Renneville, Marne, in the 1950s, and Bucy-le-Long, Aisne, in the 1970s). J. de Baye, 'Une sépulture de femme à l'époque gauloise dans la Marne', *Rev. Arch.* (1885) 70–78; A. Thenot, 'La sépulture gauloise de Bussy-le-Château, dite de "La Cheppe" (Marne)', *Bull. Soc. Préhist. Française* 72 (1975) 457–66; also, *Manuel* fig. 571, no. 2 (pendant), figs. 533, no. 13 and 534, no. 3 (two brooches).

104 Bronze jewellery, La Tène I
Villeseneux (Marne). Torque (D 168mm), two brooches with coral on the feet (L 66mm), two other brooches (L 61, 53mm), two bracelets (D 73, 72mm). M.A.N. 14952B–14958B.
This group, excavated by A. Brisson and A. Loppin in 1936, was formerly in Epernay Museum. P.-M. Favret, 'La nécropole gauloise de Villeseneux (canton de Vertus, Marne)', *Bull. Soc. Préhist. Française* 47 (1950) 433–48 (tombe 4), fig. 10, no. 1 (torque), fig. 8 (brooches), and fig. 10, no. 5 (decorated bracelet).

105 Group of jewellery, La Tène I
La Croix-en-Champagne (Marne). Bronze torque (D 143mm), pair of bronze bracelets (D 60mm), pendant comprising two amber beads, a bronze bead and the perforated tooth of a wolf. M.A.N. 67818.

106 Group of bronze jewellery, La Tène I
Vert-la-Gravelle (Marne). Torque, a complete ring without terminals (D 238mm), bracelet (D 72mm), and a pair of brooches (L 75mm) linked by a bronze chain (L 305mm). M.A.N. 67926. *Champagne* pl. 29 (torque), and p. 70, no. 4 (bracelet). (PLATE 10)

107 Bronze jewellery, La Tène I
Marson (Marne). Torque (D 141mm), two bracelets (D 74, 69mm), three brooches (L 61, 56, 51mm), and a finger-ring (D 25mm). B.M. ML.1527, 1539, 2071, 1524, 1531, 1534, 1526. CS 15–16, pl. 3, fig. 4 (torque), fig. 20 (bracelet), figs. 2, 12 and 15 (brooches), and fig. 4 (finger-ring).

108 Group of jewellery, La Tène I
Somme-Suippes (Marne). Bronze torque (D 140mm), shale bracelet (D 72mm), bronze brooch with glass or amber on foot (L 65mm), bronze brooch (L 53mm), bronze ring (D 25mm). M.A.N. 67946. *Champagne* pl. 46, no. 1 (torque).

109 Reconstructed grave-group, La Tène I
Le Mesnil-lès-Hurlus (Marne). This grave-group has been reconstructed, with a skeleton, at the entrance to the exhibition. Bronze torque (D 135mm), pair of bronze bracelets (D 70mm), replica of a gold finger-ring (D 21mm), two bronze brooches, one with a bead of coral on the foot (L 63, 46mm), and two handmade pots – a globular jar with pedestalled base (H 268mm) and a tripartite carinated jar (H 260mm). B.M. ML.1746–51, 2857, 2626. CS pl. 41, figs. 1 to 8; M. E. Mariën, *Le Groupe de la Haine* (1961) fig. 61.

110 Bronze jewellery, La Tène I
Somme-Suippes (Marne). Torque (D 145mm), bracelet (D 67mm), and a pair of brooches (L 51, 53mm). M.A.N. 67944. *Champagne* pl. 69, no. 2 (bracelet).

111 Group of bronze jewellery, La Tène I
Mareuil-le-Port (Marne). Torque (D 160mm), bracelet (D 65mm), a pair of brooches (L 81mm), and a pendant (L 50mm). M.A.N. 67889. J. de Baye, 'Cimetière gaulois de Mareuil-le-Port (Marne)', *Bull. Arch.* (1884) 66–8; *Champagne* pl. 49, no. 2 (torque), pl. 68, no. 3 (bracelet), and pl. 2, no. 6 (a brooch). (PLATE 10)

112 Group of jewellery, La Tène II
Somsois (Marne). Bronze torque (D 122mm), bronze
bracelet (D 64mm), pair of bronze anklets (D 84mm),
pair of bronze brooches (L 59mm, feet broken),
bronze belt-chain (L 1080mm, as displayed), six amber
beads, of which only three survive; the remains of an
iron brooch have not survived. B.M. ML.1564, 1939,
1567 (two), 1574, 1575, 1549, 1553. CS pl. 17, figs. 8,
15, 3 and 14; pl. 18, figs. 6 and 7; pl. 16, figs. 1 and 5.
(PLATE 11)

113 Bronze figurine of a Gaulish woman,
Roman Imperial
Found in France. H 56mm. B.M. (Greek & Roman
Antiquities) 67.5–8.748. Walters, *op. cit.*, no. 819.
(PLATE 12)

Women were not alone in wearing jewellery, for both
brooches and bracelets are found in the same graves as
weapons. Very few of the human skeletons have been
adequately studied, so that the sex of an individual is
usually established by the associated grave-goods.
Weapons are assumed always to accompany men, and it
seems that in Champagne torques are always found with
women. As early as 1884 Auguste Nicaise published a
survey that he had carried out amongst the early excavators in Champagne and confirmed that never had
torques and weapons been found with the same skeleton;
subsequent research has not altered this conclusion.
However, this does not enable all the La Tène skeletons
found in Champagne to be sexed, for more than half the
burials lacked both weapons and torques. Other jewellery
includes anklets (no. 112), pendants (nos 105 and 287),
ear-rings (nos 118 and 119) and finger-rings (no. 120), but
these items are found only rarely.

114 Six bronze bracelets, La Tène I
Département Marne, from different graves. D 60, 51,
51, 54, 65, 57mm. M.A.N. 27854 and 23039.

115 Two bronze bracelets, La Tène I
St Rémy-sur-Bussy (Marne). D 52, 77mm.
M.A.N. 20269.

116 Three bronze bracelets, La Tène II
Dixmont (Yonne). A pair of bracelets (D 115mm), and
one similar (D 110mm). M.A.N. 36006.

117 Six beads and a ring, La Tène I
Provenance unknown (Champagne). Five glass beads
(two ochre-coloured, D 19, 22mm), one amber bead
(D 33mm), and a bone ring (D 17mm). M.A.N. 20279.

118 Pair of gold ear-rings, La Tène I
Marson (Marne). D 20, 21mm. B.M. ML.1532.
CS pl. 3, fig. 13; *Manuel* fig. 542, no. 8.

119 Bronze ear-ring, La Tène I
Département Marne. D 13mm. B.M. ML.1897.
(PLATE 12)

120 Gold finger-ring, La Tène I
Somme-Bionne (Marne). D 22mm. B.M. ML.1340.
CS pl. 9, fig. 2.

Bracelets, rings and belts
Bronze belt-chains (nos 121–124) were a feature of
women's graves in La Tène II. Some were composed of a
chain of simple bronze rings ending with a hook – the
hook could engage with any of the rings and that part of
the chain not needed to encircle the waist would hang
loose and sometimes would have attached pendants.
Elaborate chains had rings alternating with bronze links
of different forms – some with enamel ornaments.
Others had bronze alternating with iron links, and where
a number of isolated bronze rings have survived con-
necting lengths of leather may be assumed. In the earlier
La Tène phase belt-hooks are known from the graves of
both men and women (nos 129 and 239). Some were
elaborately decorated, and all seem to have been fixed to
belts otherwise made entirely of leather.

121 Bronze belt with pendants, La Tène II
Wargemoulin (Marne). With enamel ornament on the
hook. L 910mm. M.A.N. 63948. F. Henry, 'Emailleurs
d'occident', *Préhistoire* 2 (1933) 65–146, fig. 3, no. 2
(bottom).

**122 Bronze belt with enamel ornament on the
links,** La Tène II
Flavigny (Marne). L 940mm. M.A.N. 67872. J. de Baye,
'Sépultures gauloises de Flavigny', *Rev. Arch.* ii, (1877),
40–46, pl. xiv, no. 1; Henry, *op. cit.*, fig. 3, no. 2
(centre).

123 Part of a bronze belt, La Tène II
Provenance unknown (Champagne). L 220mm.
B.M. ML.1902.

124 Bronze hook and rings of a belt, La Tène II
Département Marne or Ardennes. D 25–30mm.
M.A.N. 80176A.

125 Bronze belt-hook, La Tène II
Somme-Suippes (Marne). L 83mm. M.A.N. 67950.
Champagne pl. 81, no. 1.

126 Bronze belt-hook, La Tène II
Argers (Marne). L 45mm. M.A.N. 67884.

127 Bronze belt-hook with enamel decoration,
La Tène II
Camp de Châlons (Marne). L 63mm. M.A.N. 13629.
Henry, *op. cit.*, fig. 4, no. 1.

128 Bronze belt-hook, La Tène II
Bussy-le-Château (Marne). L 54mm. M.A.N. 13274.

129 Bronze hook from a leather belt, La Tène I
Beine (Marne). L 43mm. M.A.N. 80089A.
(PLATE 12)

Brooches
Brooches (nos 130–148) are frequently found in graves
of both men and women, where their normal position,
near the shoulder, suggests that they were used for
fastening a cloak. In La Tène times the gradual change in
the form of the brooch can be demonstrated by observing
the development of the foot – that part of the brooch
beyond the catchplate. A typological progression can be
traced from an upturned foot, to one curved back towards
the bow (La Tène I, no. 130), and then clasped to the bow
(La Tène II, no. 131). In the final stage (La Tène III,
no. 132) the foot is attached to the bow in the casting, and
this particular specimen retains as a moulding on the bow
a survival of the earlier clasped foot. Within this general
sequence there was a great variety of types, some local and
others more widespread in their distribution, and the
changing fashion provides one of the clearest guides to
chronology for La Tène cultures.

130 Bronze brooch, La Tène I
Provenance unknown. L 73mm. B.M. ML.2127.

131 Bronze brooch, La Tène II
Département Marne or Ardennes. L 101mm.
M.A.N. 80156.

132 Bronze brooch, La Tène III
Provenance unknown. L 79mm. B.M. W.T.812.

133 Pair of bronze brooches, linked by a chain,
La Tène I
Bergères-lès-Vertus (Marne). L (brooches) 69mm,
(chain) 320mm. M.A.N. 12006.

134 Bronze brooch linked to a ring by a chain,
La Tène I
Bussy-le-Château (Marne). L (brooch) 56mm, (ring)
32mm, (chain) 154mm. M.A.N. 22158. *Champagne* pl.
3, no. 9. (PLATE 29)

**135 Bronze brooch with a bead of coral on top of
the foot,** Late Hallstatt
Marson (Marne). L 31mm. B.M. ML.1544.

136 Bronze brooch with a duck-head at either end,
La Tène I
Caurel (Marne). L 55mm. M.A.N. 80030. *Champagne*
pl. 15, no. 7. (PLATE 13)

137 Bronze brooch, La Tène I
Cuperly (Marne). L 74mm. M.A.N. 12965. *Champagne*
pl. 11, no. 6. The name 'Marzabotto' is now firmly
established for this class of brooch, although the
example from the type-site is atypical, L. Kruta Poppi,
'Les Celtes à Marzabotto (province de Bologna)',
Etudes Celtiques 14 (1975) 345–76.

138 Bronze brooch with coral ornament, La Tène I
St Etienne-au-Temple (Marne). L 61mm. M.A.N.
12828. *Champagne* pl. 10, no. 11. A 'Münsingen'
brooch, named after a cemetery in Switzerland where
the type is well represented, F. R. Hodson, *The La
Tène cemetery at Münsingen-Rain* (Acta Bernensia, v)
(1968). (PLATE 29)

139 Bronze brooch with coral ornament, La Tène I
Département Marne. L 63mm. M.A.N. 20272.

140 Iron brooch with coral ornament, La Tène I
Camp de Châlons (Marne). L 58mm. M.A.N. 13377.

141 Bronze brooch, La Tène I
Reims (Marne). L 64mm. M.A.N. 20250. *Champagne*
pl. 13, no. 6 (provenance given as Suippes). A 'Dux'
brooch, named after a hoard in Czechoslovakia where
at least 850 brooches were found, many of them of this
type, V. Kruta, *Le trésor de Duchcov* (1971).

142 Bronze brooch, La Tène I
Somme-Suippes (Marne). L 62mm. M.A.N. 20272.

143 Bronze brooch, La Tène I
Département Marne. L 59mm. M.A.N. 27858.

144 Bronze brooch, La Tène I
L'Epine (Marne). L 46mm. M.A.N. 13028. *Champagne*
pl. 10, no. 10.

145 Bronze brooch, La Tène II
Somsois (Marne). L 59mm. B.M. ML.1573. *CS* pl. 18,
fig. 5.

146 Iron brooch, La Tène II
Quincieux (Isère). L 89mm. B.M. 50.1–17.93.

147 Bronze brooch, Augustan-Claudian
Provenance unknown (probably Champagne).
L 79mm. B.M. ML.4074. A 'Colchester' brooch, so
called because many examples were found during the
excavation of an Iron Age and Early Roman settlement
there in the 1930s, C.F.C. Hawkes & M. R. Hull,
Camulodunum (Research Rep. of the Soc. Ant. London,
no. xiv) (1947).

148 Bronze *Kragenfibel* (collar-brooch),
Augustan-Tiberian
Clamanges (Marne). Found with the shield-boss,
no. 99. L 80mm. M.A.N. 1657 BL. (PLATE 13)

Torques

To some extent a typological development of torques (neck-rings) can be established, but it is not as useful as that of the brooches. Unlike brooches, torques are not particularly common in a European context, although vast numbers are known from the graves in Champagne (nos 149–162). In so far as there is a typological progression it is from the version with small buffer terminals (no. 153) to that with massive terminals (no. 156), but many others occur. In Late Hallstatt times the hollow tubular torque with engraved decoration was popular (no. 149). Early in the La Tène period there were true torsion torques, made of a twisted strand of metal, sometimes two strands twisted together, and it was to this type that the word 'torque' was first applied. They had buffer terminals, hook-and-eye fastenings (no. 151), and some were completely annular (no. 157). Another distinctive variety in Champagne had projecting decoration (nos 158–160), particularly three projections arranged symmetrically around the circumference. Of the latter there are examples with movable sectors (no. 67), so that the torque could readily be removed, in contrast to the vast majority which seem to have been intended to remain on the neck night and day. Constant removing would soon weaken the metal, yet very few torques have been repaired (no. 156). It is likely that they served for many years, and examples with much of the decoration worn away through use have been noted on the skeletons of elderly women.

149 Bronze tubular torque, Late Hallstatt
Wargemoulin (Marne). D 155mm. B.M. ML.1705. CS pl. 36, fig. 9.

150 Iron torque, La Tène I
Marson (Marne). D 148mm. B.M. ML.1506. CS pl. 2, fig. 2; *Manuel* fig. 515, no. 2.

151 Bronze twisted torque, La Tène I
Bergères-lès-Vertus (Marne). D 157mm. B.M. ML.1583. CS pl. 21, fig. 3.

152 Bronze torque made of two twisted strands,
La Tène I
Département Marne. D 118mm. M.A.N. 20271.

153 Bronze torque with small buffer terminals,
La Tène I
Provenance unknown (Champagne). D 150mm. B.M. ML.1761.

154 Bronze torque, La Tène I
Bussy-le-Château. Larger terminals, body slightly twisted. D 155mm. M.A.N. 8324.

155 Bronze torque, La Tène I
Prosnes (Marne). D 135mm. M.A.N. 33330.

156 Bronze torque with relief ornament, La Tène I
Somme-Suippes (Marne). D 140mm. M.A.N. 67945. From the Baye collection, associated with the bracelet, no. 68.

157 Bronze torque, La Tène I
Gourgançon (Marne). Annular, with relief ornament. D 159mm. M.A.N. 1954 BL. Formerly in Epernay Museum. A. Brisson & A. Loppin, 'Les nécropoles de Gourgançon (Marne)', *Bull. Soc. Arch. Champenoise* (1938) 128–32 (tombe 7), fig. ii; *Champagne* pl. 48, no. 5, and pl. 183, nos 1 and 2.

158 Bronze torque with projecting ornament,
La Tène I
Bussy-le-Château (Marne). D 242mm. M.A.N. 13200. For the type, *Champagne* pl. 55.

159 Bronze torque with projecting ornament,
La Tène I
Provenance unknown (Champagne). D 170mm. M.A.N. 17741. For the type, P.-M. Favret & J. Prieur, 'Les torques ternaires de La Tène I en Champagne', *Rev. Arch. de l'Est et du Centre-Est* I (1950) 11–21; *Champagne* pl. 56. (PLATE 14)

160 Bronze torque with three projecting ornaments, La Tène I
Somme-Suippes (Marne). D 158mm, M.A.N. 33333. For the type, Favret & Prieur *op. cit.*; *Champagne* pl. 57.

161 Bronze torque with duck and wheel ornament,
La Tène I
Somme-Tourbe (Marne). D 200mm. M.A.N. 12985. *Champagne* pl. 61, no. 2; *ECA* no. 239; for the type, D. Bretz-Mahler, 'Les torques ornithomorphes de La Tène I', *Bull. Soc. Préhist. Française* 56 (1959) 493–9.

162 Part of a bronze torque with duck and wheel ornament, La Tène I
Provenance unknown (Champagne). L 137mm. B.M. ML.2202. (PLATE 14)

Pottery

Pottery was frequently placed in the graves of both men and women, and its purpose seems to have been to hold food and drink for the dead. No significance for the choice of vessels or their position in the grave has yet been deduced. Only a limited range of forms was placed in burials; cooking-pots and storage jars, which occur in quantity on settlement sites, are rare. Funerary wares were limited to the more skilfully finished decorative eating and drinking vessels. Some of the finest types have never been found in domestic contexts and so may have been produced exclusively for burials.

In the La Tène I period, most graves held up to five

pots, although some spectacular burials have more, and include many of the largest and finest decorated forms. The elegant shouldered jars with tall pedestalled bases (nos 43 and 185) were made on a fast-turning wheel, but the majority were shaped by hand, with varying degrees of skill and success. The finest were pared down on a turn-table to produce thin-walled shapes with sharp carinations and acute angles (no. 173). The surfaces were burnished smooth both inside and out, and some were decorated with painted or incised geometric patterns. Most were fired to a glossy dark grey or brown colour in smoky oxygen-starved conditions. Red pots were produced by coating the surface with haematite or other iron oxides combined with controlled firing. Elaborate permanent kilns were not necessary, and none has yet been found in Champagne, although some specialist potters must have been at work. Nos 163–185 are arranged typologically, and nos 186–188 are La Tène I burial groups.

Relatively few burials have been assigned to La Tène II, and so there is comparatively little La Tène II pottery. The wheel continued to be used for pedestalled bowls and jars like nos 193 and 197, although most pots were still handmade. The wheel may have added impetus to the development of specialist full-time potters, while it also affected the shapes produced, leading to the disappearance of the angular La Tène I forms. Decoration now included burnished patterns on a contrasting matt background (no. 193).

163 Cylindrical beaker, La Tène I
Provenance unknown (Champagne). Handmade.
H 72mm. B.M. ML.2789.

164 Small beaker, La Tène I
St Etienne-au-Temple (Marne). Handmade. H 60mm.
M.A.N. 5020.

165 Bowl, La Tène I
St Etienne-au-Temple (Marne). Handmade. H 48mm.
M.A.N. 15396.

166 Biconical carinated dish, La Tène I
Département Marne. Handmade. H 52mm.
M.A.N. 23043. (PLATE 15)

167 Biconical carinated jar, La Tène I
Marson (Marne). Handmade. H 180mm. B.M. ML.2860.
CS pl. 41, fig. 17. (PLATE 15)

168 Biconical carinated jar, La Tène I
Bergères-lès-Vertus (Marne). Handmade. H 144mm.
B.M. ML.2659. CS pl. 41, fig. 22.

169 Tripartite carinated beaker, La Tène I
Suippes (Marne). Handmade. H 72mm. B.M. ML.2733.
(PLATE 15)

170 Tripartite carinated beaker, La Tène I
Le Mesnil-lès-Hurlus (Marne). Handmade. H 90mm.
B.M. ML.2719.

171 Tripartite carinated beaker, La Tène I
La Croix-en-Champagne (Marne). Handmade.
H 112mm. B.M. ML.2708. (PLATE 15)

172 Tripartite carinated goblet, La Tène I
Marson (Marne). Handmade. H 112mm.
B.M. ML.2627. CS pl. 41, fig. 10. (PLATE 15)

173 Tripartite carinated bowl, La Tène I
Marson (Marne). Handmade. H 174mm. B.M. ML.2633.
CS pl. 4, fig. 3 and pl. 41, fig. 23. (PLATE 15)

174 Tripartite carinated bowl, La Tène I
Marson (Marne). Handmade. H 132mm. B.M. ML.2632.
CS pl. 41, fig. 21. (PLATE 15)

175 Tripartite carinated jar, La Tène I
La Croix-en-Champagne (Marne). Handmade
H 125mm. M.A.N. 12491.

176 Tripartite carinated jar, La Tène I
Département Aisne. Handmade. H 405mm. M.A.N.
(no registration no.). (PLATE 16)

177 Tripartite carinated jar, La Tène I
St Jean-sur-Tourbe (Marne). Handmade. H 370mm.
M.A.N. 27639.

178 Ovoid jar, La Tène I
Prosnes (Marne). Handmade. H 212mm. B.M. ML.2671.
CS pl. 24, fig. 26.

179 Ovoid beaker, La Tène I
Somme-Bionne (Marne). Handmade. H 96mm.
CS pl. 15, fig. 8.

180 Tulip-shaped beaker, La Tène I
Etrechy (Marne). Handmade. H 280mm. M.A.N. 75396.

181 Tulip-shaped goblet, La Tène I
Fontaine-en-Dormois (Marne). Handmade. H 156mm.
B.M. ML.2728. (PLATE 16)

182 Tulip-shaped goblet, La Tène I
Bussy-le-Château (Marne). Handmade. H 132mm.
B.M. ML.2697 (PLATE 16)

183 Tulip-shaped beaker, La Tène I
Ciry-Salsogne (Aisne). Handmade. H 138mm.
M.A.N. 42442. (PLATE 16)

184 Tulip-shaped goblet, La Tène I
Provenance unknown (Champagne). Handmade.
H 268mm. B.M. ML.2840. (PLATE 16)

185 Shouldered jar with hollow pedestalled base,
La Tène I
Somme-Bionne (Marne). Wheelmade. H 256mm.
B.M. ML.1334. CS pl. 15, fig. 11. (PLATE 17)

186 A burial group of four handmade vessels,
La Tène I
Witry-lès-Reims (Marne). Two biconical dishes
(H 45mm), a tripartite carinated beaker (H 87mm), and
a necked and shouldered jar (H 228mm). M.A.N. 23031.
(PLATE 17).

187 A burial group of two handmade vessels,
La Tène I
Witry-lès-Reims (Marne). A biconical dish (H 45mm),
and a necked and shouldered jar (H 153mm). M.A.N.
23009.

188 A burial group of three vessels, La Tène I
Witry-lès-Reims (Marne). A biconical carinated dish
(H 36mm), a beaker (H 90mm), and a necked and
shouldered jar (H 225mm). M.A.N. 23009.

189 Shouldered bowl, La Tène II
Gournay-sur-Aronde (Oise). Handmade. H49mm.
M.A.N. 28526. J.-C. Blanchet & A. Duval, 'Les
collections de La Tène provenant de l'Oise et de la
Somme au Musée des Antiquités Nationales',
Antiquités Nationales 7 (1975) 51, fig. 3, no. 4.

190 Shouldered bowl, La Tène II
Département Marne or Ardennes. Wheelmade.
H 107mm. M.A.N. 80155.

191 Shouldered bowl, La Tène II
Provenance unknown (Champagne). Wheelmade.
H 145mm. M.A.N. 46913.

192 Shouldered bowl, La Tène II
Somme-Tourbe (Marne). Wheelmade. H 148mm.
B.M. ML.2712. (PLATE 18)

193 Shouldered and carinated bowl, La Tène II
Marson (Marne). Wheelmade. H 232mm. B.M.
ML.1504. CS pl. 1, fig. 7. (PLATE 18)

194 Biconical jar, La Tène I/II
Département Marne. Handmade. H 150mm.
M.A.N. 80153. (PLATE 18)

195 Shouldered jar with incised decoration,
La Tène II
Provenance unknown (Champagne or Picardy).
Handmade. H 145mm. M.A.N. 83526.

**196 Shouldered jar with trumpet-shaped
pedestalled base,** La Tène II
St Etienne-au-Temple (Marne). Wheelmade.
H 277mm. M.A.N. 12880. (PLATE 18)

197 Shouldered jar with pedestalled foot,
La Tène I/II
Somme-Bionne (Marne). Wheelmade. H 272mm.
B.M. ML.1336.

198 Shouldered jar, La Tène II/III
Armentières (Aisne). Wheelmade. H 315mm.
M.A.N. 42299. (PLATE 19)

The wine trade

A passion for wine, well illustrated by finds from the
graves, is confirmed by ancient historians: 'They are
exceedingly fond of wine and sate themselves with the
unmixed wine imported by merchants; their desire makes
them drink it greedily and when they become drunk
they fall into a stupor or into a maniacal disposition. And
therefore many Italian merchants with their usual love of
lucre look on the Gallic love of wine as their treasure
trove. They transport the wine by boat on the navigable
rivers and by wagon through the plains and receive in
return for it an incredibly large price; for one jar of wine
they receive in return a slave, a servant in exchange for
the drink' (Diodorus Siculus v.26.3).

Both Greek and Italian merchants carried wine, and the
vessels needed for mixing, serving and drinking it, into
the lands of the Gauls. The Greek settlement at Massalia
(Marseille), established about 600 BC, became an important
trading centre through which Greek exports passed up the
River Rhône. Etruscan exports followed the same route,
and also made use of the Alpine passes. Gallic products
traded in the opposite direction were doubtless similar
to the British exports listed by Strabo: 'corn, cattle, gold,
silver, iron . . . together with hides, slaves and dogs useful
for hunting' (Strabo IV.5.2) – commodities which would
leave little archaeological trace.

Of the artefacts, the most common imported vessels
found in Gaulish graves are bronze beaked flagons (nos
69 and 199). They were produced in Etruscan workshops
in the period 550 to 400 BC, and about eighty of them
have been found north of the Alps, including four from
Champagne. Large Etruscan wine jars were also exported
(no. 201), and very rarely Greek pottery cups are found
(no. 69). Native forms of flagon were also made in
bronze (nos 202 and 221) and in pottery (no. 203).

199 Etruscan bronze beaked flagon, La Tène I
Probably found in Italy. H 285mm. B.M. (Greek &
Roman Antiquities) 67.5–8.726. Cf. also the flagon in
the reconstructed Somme-Bionne burial (no. 69). For
discoveries of this form in France see B. Bouloumié,
'Les oenochoes en bronze du type *Schnabelkanne* en
France et en Belgique', *Gallia* 31 (1973) 1–35.

200 Part of the handle of a bronze Etruscan jar,
Late Hallstatt
Bourges (Cher). H (of animal) 43mm. B.M. ML.1620.
CS pl. 25, fig. 2; for the type see L. Lerat, 'L'amphore
de bronze de Conliège (Jura)', (Actes du colloque sur
les influences hellenique en Gaule), *Pubs. Université de
Dijon* 16 (1958) 89–98. (PLATE 19)

201 Etruscan bronze jar, La Tène I
Basse-Yutz (Moselle). Found with another similar
vessel and the two fine Celtic flagons (no. 221).
H 379mm. B.M. 1929 5–11 3. R. A. Smith, 'Celtic
bronzes from Lorraine', *Arch.* 79 (1929) 1–12.

202 Bronze spouted flagon, La Tène I
St Jean-sur-Tourbe (Marne). H 330mm. M.A.N. 27357
E. Fourdrignier, 'Le vase de bronze du Catillon', *Rev.
Arch.* ii (1883), 201–4; *Manuel* fig. 654, no. 2; *ECA*
no. 389. (PLATE 19)

203 Pottery spouted flagon, La Tène I
Poix (Marne). H 215mm. M.A.N. 77065. L. Bérard,
'Nécropole gauloise de Poix (Marne)', *Bull, Soc. Arch.
Champenoise* (1914) 12–24, fig. 19, tombe 41;
Champagne pl. 120, no. 2; *ECA* no. 407. (PLATE 20)

The Gallic War

Napoléon III was particularly interested in the conflict between the Gauls and Julius Caesar, and promoted excavation and fieldwork on and around some of the major Gallic strongholds (oppida). Caesar defeated the Gauls in a series of campaigns between 58 and 50 BC, and published his version of the events, including detailed descriptions of oppida and battlefields. Napoléon was keen to identify these sites on the ground, and to recognise both native and Roman earthworks. Some oppida, for instance Avaricum (Bourges), were identified without difficulty, but others, such as Bibracte (Mont Beuvray) and particularly Alesia, presented more of a problem. Napoléon identified Alesia with Mont Auxois, Alise-Sainte-Reine, Côte d'Or, and was subsequently proved correct, but the supporters of a rival site, Alaise, Doubs, carried on a heated academic battle for many years. Napoléon's excavations were concentrated on the Plaine des Laumes, to the west of Mont Auxois, where he identified Caesarian camps and siege-works and recovered a quantity of weapons (no. 214). This was the setting for the last stand of the Gauls, under the leadership of Vercingetorix, and the fall of Alesia marked the end of Gallic independence. Vercingetorix was honoured by a huge bronze statue, erected on the heights of Mont Auxois in 1865 by an admiring emperor whose drooping features might have been used as the model for the hero's face.

Many oppida were defended by a wall whose distinctive construction, described by Caesar, has now entered archaeological vocabulary as a *murus Gallicus*. Such walls were built of timber and stone, the timber being arranged only in horizontal layers, first across the line of the wall and then along it, to form a framework. The cross-timbers were set at intervals of about a metre and were joined at right-angles by three or four long-timbers, sometimes up to thirteen metres long. The framework was filled with rubble and earth, and faced with a stone revetment which the cross-timbers penetrated. This construction greatly impressed Caesar: 'this work is not unsightly in appearance and variety, with alternate balks (of timber) and stones which keep their proper courses in straight lines; and it is eminently suitable for the practical defence of cities, since the stone protects from fire and the timber from battery, for with continuous balks generally forty feet long made fast on the inside it can neither be breached nor pulled to pieces' (Caesar, *De Bello Gallico* VII.23). One of the distinctive features of the *murus Gallicus* is the use of massive iron nails to link the timbers (no. 215).

Celtic oppida were walled towns with extensive occupation inside. Mont Beuvray (Bibracte) was selected by Napoléon III for systematic excavation, and in 1867 he appointed Gabriel Bulliot to take charge. Bulliot was eventually succeeded in this post by his nephew, Joseph Déchelette, an outstanding European archaeologist and the author of the magnificent *Manuel*, a work of synthesis which is still unsurpassed. Déchelette was later killed at the head of his company little more than two months after the outbreak of the First World War, fighting for his country, at the age of fifty-three. The La Tène volume of the *Manuel* was published in that same year, and by that time Mont Beuvray had produced so much material that it could be regarded as the type-site for the La Tène III period. Indeed, more than twenty years previously Gabriel de Mortillet had divided the La Tène period into two phases, *marnien* (after the Champagne burials) and *beuvraysien*. Much of the occupation of Mont Beuvray belongs to the post-Caesarian period, and it ceases completely in the reign of Augustus.

Nos 204–211, La Tène III pottery from Mont Beuvray (Saône-et-Loire/Nievre – the departmental boundary crosses the site), were found on Bulliot's excavations, (see G. Bulliot, *Fouilles de Mont Beuvray 1867 à 1895* (1899)).

204 Sherd with rouletted decoration
H 95mm. M.A.N. 17966.

205 Sherd with graffito
H 49mm. M.A.N. 24293.

206 Platter
Wheelmade. H 35mm. M.A.N. 17345.

207 Platter
Wheelmade. H 35mm. M.A.N. 17347.

208 Dish
H 47mm. M.A.N. 17352.

209 Bowl
Wheelmade. H 55mm. M.A.N. 17352.

210 Bowl
Wheelmade. H 75mm. M.A.N. 24285.

211 Non-spill bowl
Handmade. H 65mm. M.A.N. 17571.

212-13 Bowl and group of sherds with painted decoration, La Tène III
Provenance unknown. Wheelmade, examples of Roanne painted wares. M.A.N. 83616 & 83617.

214 Four iron spear-heads, La Tène III
Mont Auxois, Alise-Sainte-Reine (Côte-d'Or). Found during Napoléon III's excavations in 1869. L 270, 220, 244, 353mm. M.A.N. 10118, 10114, 10109, 10094.

215 Five iron nails used in a *murus Gallicus*, La Tène III
Luzech (Lot). L (longest) 310mm. M.A.N. 24499. Luzech, which has claims to be Uxellodunum, was an oppidum of the Cadurci. The nails were excavated by Castagné in 1872. For a general account of *muri Gallici* see M. A. Cotton's appendix to Sir Mortimer Wheeler & K. M. Richardson, *Hill-forts of Northern France* (Reports of the Research Committee of the Society of Antiquaries of London, xix) (1957) 159–225.

216 A pot, glass cup and coin, found together, La Tène III
Corent (Puy-de-Dôme). A replica of the coin is displayed. M.A.N. 31874. Corent is a hill-top oppidum which has not been systematically excavated, *Manuel* 957–8.

217 Five miniature bronze wheels, La Tène III
Mont Chaté, Boviolles (Meuse). Mounted on bronze wire. D 15mm. M.A.N. 8917. Mont Chaté was an oppidum of the Leuci and had *murus Gallicus* defences, Cotton, *op. cit.*, 204–5. Miniature wheels in gold, bronze and lead were found here in the nineteenth century, including a hoard of 38 associated with 19 Gallic coins, *Dictionnaire Archéologique de la Gaule*, i (1875) 190.

218 Bronze key, La Tène III
Near Chalon-sur-Saône (Saône-et-Loire). L 68mm. M.A.N. 71488. For the type see *Manuel* fig. 619, no. 6, and 620, no. 2.

219 Glass jewellery, La Tène III
Mathay (Doubs). Fourteen glass beads on a bronze ring, three glass bracelets (D 86, 75, 65mm), and two glass rings (D 31, 17mm). M.A.N. 52491. *Manuel* 1327, note 3.

220 Glass bracelet, La Tène III
Provenance unknown (possibly Champagne). D 85mm. M.A.N. 83289.

Celtic Art

Basse-Yutz

The various roots of Celtic art can be demonstrated by studying the remarkable pair of highly decorated flagons from Basse-Yutz (no. 221). Although an element of mystery surrounds their discovery, they were probably found in a rich grave, but one which was sited well to the east of Champagne and which relates more closely to the Early La Tène burials of the middle Rhineland. These two areas, Champagne and the middle Rhineland, were major centres of Early La Tène culture, best known from burials: the finds from some of the Rhenish burials are even more spectacular than those from Champagne. The earliest manifestations of Celtic art, the Early Style, are seen on objects in rich burials in these two groups, where they appear not as a gradual development from earlier native art but as a sudden flourish relying heavily on foreign influences. One of the main roots lies in the classical world, in Greek or Etruscan art, yet La Tène art did not originate in those parts of Gaul in immediate contact with the Greeks, but in remote areas with long-distance trade links. Classical art was not slavishly copied, but the derivation of individual motifs, especially the representation of plant forms, is clear enough; such motifs were adopted, modified, dissected and elaborated to form a quite distinctive art-style. On the Basse-Yutz flagons the palmettes under the spouts and on the handles are good examples of classical influence.

A second element in La Tène art has a clear oriental flavour, but any precise source is difficult to define. Masks, and representations of animals such as those on the handles and rims of the flagons, could owe something to the Scythians or even the Persians, although there was also an oriental element in Etruscan art. Finally, La Tène art is not entirely devoid of a native root, and its Hallstatt origins are best seen in geometric forms. On the Basse-Yutz flagons there is also a duck, a popular Hallstatt motif, sitting at the source of the river of wine on each spout.

221 Pair of bronze flagons, La Tène I
Basse-Yutz (Moselle). With coral and enamel ornament. H 376, 387mm. B.M. 1929.5–11.1 and 2.
R. A. Smith, 'Celtic bronzes from Lorraine' *Arch.* 79 (1929) 1–12; *ECA* no. 381. (PLATE 21)

Early style

The new art-style is found mainly on metalwork, and especially on luxury items. It was created for the wealthy element in Gallic society, whose love of southern wine exposed them to Greek art, and whose native artists were particularly receptive to new ideas. In Champagne Greek or Etruscan influence is very apparent on a group of bronzes decorated with fine engraved ornament whose motifs are based on classical representations of plant forms – especially the palmette and lotus. These pieces were found in richly equipped cart-burials like Somme-Bionne (no. 69), with its imported Etruscan flagon and Greek cup. The tall conical helmet from Berru (no. 222) has a zone of engraved ornament at the top and another at the bottom. The design is based on a palmette with detached leaves, and a continuous frieze has been created by linking alternate upright and reversed palmettes with a curved form perhaps devolved from a lotus petal. Reference to Fig. 2 may help to explain the derivation of this motif. The Prunay helmet (no. 223) has a simple palmette device associated with geometric ornament, and like the Berru helmet it has been newly restored at Mainz. The two larger discs from Ecury-sur-Coole (no. 224; see Fig. 3) have four palmettes arranged symmetrically, whilst each of the smaller discs (no. 225) has an engraved three-part whirligig. The outlines on the smaller discs have been produced by rocking a tracer as opposed to the fine engraved lines on the other pieces. Similar rocked tracer lines were used on a helmet from the same Ecury-sur-Coole grave – it was presumably similar in form to the Berru helmet but unfortunately only fragments survive. A bronze bowl from Saulces-Champenoises (no. 226), now apparently lost and known only from a replica, was decorated in the same style, but with motifs rather more dissected. Its central tripartite whirligig is similar to that from Ecury-sur-Coole, although moving in the opposite direction (Fig. 5). Elaborate and delicate engraving covers the entire surface, including the base, of a bronze flagon now in Besançon Museum (no. 227; see Fig. 4). The flagon is an Etruscan form, but it was certainly ornamented in France. Unfortunately it lacks a provenance, although it seems very likely that it was found in a grave, perhaps not far from its present home. The pot from St Pol-de-Léon, in Brittany (no. 228), is obviously decorated in a style

Fig. 2 *The Celtic palmette:* (a) *Etruscan palmette and lotus flowers;* (b) *no. 222 (Berru);* (c) *no. 223 (Prunay);* (d) *no. 233 (Puisieulx);* (e) *no. 227 (Besançon);* (f) *no. 224 (Ecury-sur-Coole);* (g) *no. 228 (St Pol-de-Léon);* (h) *and* (j) *no. 255 (Cerrig-y-drudion);* (k) *no. 221 (Basse-Yutz);* (l) *no. 229 (Somme-Tourbe);* (m) *no. 230 (Mairy-sur-Marne).*

Fig. 3 *The design on one of the discs from Ecury-sur-Coole, no. 224 (after Champion).*

Fig. 4 *The design on the Bescançon flagon, no. 227 (after Frey).*

reminiscent of the metalwork from eastern France, and also has striking similarities with the bronze fragments from Cerrig-y-drudion in Wales (no. 255).

222 Bronze helmet, La Tène I
Berru (Marne). H 295mm. M.A.N. 20583. E. de Barthélemy, 'Note sur une sépulture antique fouillée à Berru (Marne) en 1872', *Mems. Soc. Ant. France* 35 (1874) 92–8; A. Bertrand, 'Le casque de Berru', *Rev. Arch.* (1875) 244–53; *Manuel* fig. 490, no. 2 and fig. 656; *ECA* no. 136. (PLATE 22)

223 Bronze helmet, La Tène I
Prunay (Marne). H 165mm. Musée St Remi, Reims, 978–16162. P. Coulon, 'Note sur un casque gaulois recueilli dans le cimetière des Marquises, près Prunay (Marne)', *Bull. Soc. Arch. Champenoise* (1930) 44–5; *ECA* no. 139. (PLATE 22)

224 Two bronze discs backed by iron crosses, La Tène I
Ecury-sur-Coole (Marne). D 172, 143mm. M.A.N. 77050. A. Thierot, 'Fond de cabane de l'époque hallstattienne, cimetières celtiques, tombe gallo-romaine, des "Côtes-en-Marne" à Ecury-sur-Coole', *Bull. Soc. Arch. Champenoise* (1931) 38–56, fig. p. 45; *ECA* no. 189 (the drawings, pl. 117, by Champion).

225 Two smaller bronze discs from the same grave, La Tène I
Ecury-sur-Coole (Marne). D 59mm. M.A.N. 77050. Thierot, *op. cit.*; *ECA* no. 189. (PLATE 22)

226 Replica of a bronze bowl, La Tène I
Saulces-Champenoises (Ardennes). D 280mm. M.A.N. 63945. Excavated by Courty, *Bull. Soc. Arch. Champenoise* (1912) 97, and acquired by Bérard for his private collection; now lost. Reinach called it the 'vase Bérard' and had this replica made, *Rev. Arch.* i (1918), 182. Bérard's drawing is reproduced in *Manuel* fig. 655; *ECA* pl. 249b.

227 Bronze flagon, La Tène I
Provenance unknown. H 255mm. Musée des
Beaux-Arts, Besançon. O. H. Frey, 'Eine etruskische
Bronzeschnabelkanne im Museum von Besançon',
Annales Littéraires de l'Université de Besançon,
Archéologie 2 (1955). (PLATE 22)

228 Shouldered jar, La Tène I
St Pol-de-Léon (Finistère). Handmade. H 260mm.
Musée des Jacobins, Morlaix, 74–127. P. du Chatelier,
*La Poterie aux Epoques préhistoire et gauloise en
Armorique* (1897), pl. 14, fig. 1, 2 & p. 53; *Manuel*,
fig. 663, no. 1; *ECA* pl. 278, no. 470. (PLATE 23)

Fine engraving was not the only means of executing
classical-derived ornament on objects from the Champagne cart-burials. The heavy 'horn-cap' from Somme-
Tourbe (no. 229) and the thin bronze plaque from
Mairy-sur-Marne (no. 230) bear the same device, two
linked palmettes, one upright and the other reversed, but
the execution is quite different, for the design on the
Mairy piece is formed by repoussé work (hammering
from the underside) whereas the motif on the 'horn-cap'
was apparently cast. On the opposite side of the 'horn-cap'
another palmette has been finely engraved. A bronze
object from the same grave at Somme-Tourbe (no. 231)
has a cut-out design repeating a 'lyre' – opposed s-forms –
and a similar device alternates with a 'running-dog'
(which also appears on the top-knot of the Berru helmet,
no. 222) round the cut-out border of a large disc from
St Jean-sur-Tourbe (no. 232). Designs derived from the
palmette are also found on pottery (nos 233 and 234);
painted pottery is rare in La Tène I, and these two examples
should be compared with the jar from Prunay (no. 241).

229 Bronze terminal of a cart-pole, La Tène I
'La Bouvandeau', Somme-Tourbe (Marne).
L 145mm. M.A.N. 33295. E. Flouest, 'Le char de la
sépulture gauloise de la Bouvandeau, commune de
Somme-Tourbe (Marne)', *Mems. Soc. Ant. France* 46
(1885) 99–111; *Manuel* fig. 692; *ECA* no. 168 (refers to
traces of red enamel in the circular ornaments).

230 Bronze plaque, La Tène I
Mairy-sur-Marne (Marne). L 70mm. M.A.N. 77055.
From Burial 200, a cart-burial, in the Mairy-Sogny
cemetery: L. Bérard, 'Cimetière gaulois de Mairy-
Sogny', *Bull. Soc. Arch. Champenoise* (1914) 109–20,
where it is listed but not illustrated; *Champagne* pl. 134,
no. 2; *ECA* no. 379 (gives the burial as no. 47).
(PLATE 23)

231 Bronze object with cut-out ornament,
La Tène I
'La Bouvandeau', Somme-Tourbe (Marne). The
decoration of a cart-pole or yoke. L 183mm. M.A.N.
33294. One of a pair of objects. Flouest, *op. cit.*,

considered them as part of the cart-pole with no. 229
here (his illustration is repeated in *Manuel* fig. 505);
M. E. Mariën, *Le Groupe de La Haine* (1961) 176,
followed by S. Piggott, 'Early Iron Age "horn-caps"
and yokes', *Antiq. Journ.* 49 (1969) 378–81, interpreted
them as fittings of a yoke – but there were iron yoke
fittings in the grave as well, Flouest, *op. cit.*, 101;
ECA no. 171 – Jacobsthal's identification of them as
hame-mountings is corrected by Piggott, *op. cit.*,
380–1. (PLATE 24)

232 Bronze disc, backed by an iron cross,
La Tène I
St Jean-sur-Tourbe (Marne). A piece of coral at the
centre of the disc. D 245mm. M.A.N. 33284. One of a
pair, excavated by J.-B. Counhaye; *ECA* no. 184.
(PLATE 24)

**233 Shouldered jar with trumpet-shaped
pedestalled base,** La Tène I
Puisieulx (Marne). H 350mm. Musée St Remi, Reims,
978–16286. P.-M. Duval, *Les Celtes* (1977) 74, fig. 60.
(PLATE 25)

**234 Shouldered jar with trumpet-shaped
pedestalled base,** La Tène I
Jonchery-sur-Suippes (Marne). H 350mm. M.A.N.
27829. A. Varagnac & G. Fabre, *L'Art Gaulois* (1956)
274, pl. 60.

Apart from its palmettes, the Somme-Tourbe 'horn-cap'
is ornamented with simple circles and arcs which recall
similar decoration, especially on pottery, in eastern
Celtic provinces such as Bavaria and Bohemia. Such
abstract, compass-constructed ornament is an important
element in Celtic art, and despite its essentially eastern
distribution the most elaborate examples are found in
Champagne. The design of the Cuperly disc (no. 235) is
based on a simple arrangement of intersecting circles, but
the cut-out bronzes from the Somme-Bionne cart-burial –
especially the circular disc (no. 236) – are much more
complex. Here interlocking circles are used to create new
shapes, whose outlines are emphasised by paired engraved
lines bordering rows of punched dots. There is similar
linear ornament on another plaque from Cuperly (no.
238), a fascinating piece whose ornament includes a
central multi-leaf palmette of classical inspiration and a
double-headed dragon which hints at eastern influence.
Fantastic animals are rare in Champagne's Celtic art, but
there is also a fine pair of confronted griffins on a belt-
terminal from Somme-Bionne (no. 239).

235 Bronze disc with enamel inlay, La Tène I
Cuperly (Marne). D 110mm. M.A.N. 27719.
E. Fourdrignier, 'Les casques gaulois à form conique:
l'influence orientale', *Congrès Arch. France* 47 (1880)
370–96 (fig. p. 378); *ECA* no. 185. (PLATE 25)

236 Bronze disc, La Tène I
Somme-Bionne (Marne). D 67mm. B.M. ML.1369.
CS pl. 10, fig. 11; *Manuel* fig. 506, no. 2; *ECA* no.
180. (PLATE 26)

237 Bronze cut-out ornament, La Tène I
Somme-Bionne (Marne). H 59mm. B.M. ML.1366.
CS pl. 10, fig. 10; *Manuel* fig. 506, no. 1; *ECA* no.
192. (PLATE 27)

238 Bronze plaque, La Tène I
Cuperly (Marne). H 91mm. M.A.N. 27719. From the
same grave as no. 235; the excavator, Fourdrignier,
thought that it decorated the front of a leather helmet,
op. cit., figs. pp. 376 and 373; *ECA* no. 200. (PLATE 27)

239 Bronze belt-terminal, La Tène I
Somme-Bionne (Marne). H 63mm. B.M. ML.1347.
CS pl. 9, fig. 5; *Manuel* fig. 524, no. 1; *ECA* no. 359;
O.-H. Frey, 'Durchbrochene Frühlatène-gürtelhaken
aus Slowenien', *Situla* 14/15 (1974) 129–42, fig. 7, no. 6.
(PLATE 28)

Later styles

The magnificent gilded helmet from Amfreville (no. 240)
stands apart from most of the other French objects
because it was not found in a grave. It was discovered in
an old channel of the River Seine and was offered by its
owner to Napoléon III, who had it displayed in the
Louvre some years before the Musée des antiquités
nationales was opened. It is important in that it introduces
a motif which was to play a significant role in the development of Early Celtic Art throughout Europe – the
tendril (Fig. 5). The central zone of decoration on the
helmet comprises a string of triangular shapes linked by
spindly tendrils which spiral from each corner. They
might be regarded as a chain of whirligigs, and indeed
the whirligigs on the smaller discs from Ecury-sur-Coole
(no. 225) are bounded by a formal symmetrical version of
this pattern. In different media, the Prunay pot (no. 241)
has a design based on a string of such triangles, and the
Prosnes brooch (no. 242) has a tendril frieze whose
terminations are triple-leaves – but the small scale of this
detail makes it difficult to display. The four-cornered
whirligig on a strainer from the Morel collection (no. 243)
has symmetrical tendrils which should be compared with
the treatment of the same motif on the base of the
Besançon flagon. This tendril-dominated style is named
after a rich grave-group at Waldalgesheim, in the middle
Rhineland, which included both native and classical
objects. Champagne is one of the few areas in Celtic
Europe where the distribution of objects decorated in the
Early Style and Waldalgesheim Style coincides, and
where there seems to be some development from the
one style to the other.

Fig. 5 *Celtic whirligigs* (a–d) *and tendrils* (e–g): (a)
no. 225 (Ecury-sur-Coole); (b) *no. 226* (Saulces-
Champenoises); (c) *no. 227* (Besançon); (d) *no. 243*
(Morel collection); (e) *no. 240* (Amfreville); (f) *no. 241*
(Prunay); (g) *no. 242* (Prosnes).

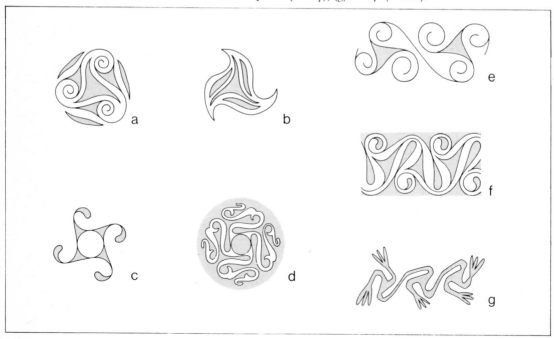

240 Bronze helmet overlaid with three decorative hoops, La Tène I
Amfreville-sous-les-Monts(Eure). Top and bottom hoops, openwork iron with enamel inlay, and between them a gilded bronze hoop. H 175mm. M.A.N. 2153. E. Viollet Le Duc, 'Casque antique trouvé dans un ancien bras de la Seine', *Rev. Arch.*, i (1862), 225–7, pl. v; *Manuel* fig. 490, no. 3; *ECA* no. 140. (PLATE 28)

241 Shouldered jar with trumpet-shaped pedestalled base, La Tène I
Prunay (Marne). H 310mm. B.M. ML.2734. *CS* fig., frontispiece, centre; *Manuel* fig. 660, no. 2,; *ECA* no. 408. (PLATE 29)

242 Bronze brooch, La Tène I
Prosnes (Marne). L 63mm. B.M. ML.1614. V. Kruta, 'Les fibules laténiennes à décor d'inspiration végétale au IVe siècle avant notre ère', *Etudes Celtiques* 15 1976–7) 19–46, fig. 4, no. 2; *CS* pl. 24, fig. 25.

243 Bronze strainer, La Tène I
Provenance unknown. D 102mm. B.M. ML.2167. *ECA* no. 400. It was no doubt used in a vessel like that found in Barrow 2 at Hoppstädten, L. Killian, 'Hügelgräber bei Hoppstädten. Ergebnisse der Grabung 1952', *Trier. Zeits.* 24–6 (1956–8) 59–102, pl. 19, no. 1. (PLATE 29)

Towards the end of La Tène I the decoration of metalwork was essentially in relief, in a freer style less restrained than the earlier engraved ornament. Some motifs are derived from Waldalgesheim tendrils, and others make use of spirals, s-forms and coils. Bronze was cast by the *cire perdue* technique, whereby a wax model was used to produce a clay mould which could be used only once to produce a bronze object. Sometimes the confrontation of s-forms gave rise to shapes resembling human heads, and occasionally, as on the Courtisols torque (no. 249) there can be no doubt about the human representation. The Tarn bracelet (no. 250) is a magnificent example of plastic art in high relief, and the ultimate in this style is seen in the group of horse-harness and vehicle fittings said to have been found near Paris (nos 251–254).

244 Bronze bracelet, La Tène I
Mareuil-le-Port (Marne). D 72mm. M.A.N. 67891. J. de Baye, 'Cimetière gaulois de Mareuil-le-Port (Marne)', *Bull. Arch.* (1884) 66–8, pl. 2c.

245 Bronze bracelet, La Tène I
Bergères-lès-Vertus (Marne). D 65mm. M.A.N. 1706 BL. Formerly in Epernay Museum; A. Brisson & Duval, 'Cimetière gaulois des "Terres de Monsieur", commune de Bergères-lès-Vertus (Marne)', *Bull. Soc. Arch. Champenoise* (1934) 48–52, fig. 2.

246 Bronze brooch, La Tène I
Selliers (Aube). L 64mm. M.A.N. (PLATE 29)

247 Bronze torque, La Tène I
Prunay (Marne). D 151mm. M.A.N. 33321. *ECA* no. 223.

248 Bronze torque, La Tène I
Avon-Fontenay (Aube). D 154mm. B.M. ML.1709. *CS* pl. 37, fig. 2; *ECA* no. 241.

249 Bronze torque, La Tène I
Courtisols (Marne). D 157mm. B.M. ML.1711. *CS* pl. 37, fig. 4; *Manuel* fig. 515, no. 6; *ECA* no. 208. (PLATE 30)

250 Bronze bracelet, La Tène II
Département Tarn. D 90mm. M.A.N. 50206. *ECA* no. 275. (PLATE 30)

251 Bronze head of an iron linch-pin, La Tène II
? Paris. W 85mm. M.A.N. 51401. *ECA* no. 163. Nos 251–254 form a group acquired from a dealer; the 'Paris' provenance is not as unlikely as Jacobsthal supposed (*ECA* p. 184); see especially A. Duval & J-C. Blanchet, 'La tombe à char d'Attichy (Oise)', *Bull. Soc. Préhist. Française* 71 (1974) 401–8. (PLATE 30)

252 Bronze terret (rein-ring), La Tène II
? Paris. H 85mm. M.A.N. 51400. *ECA* no. 175a. (PLATE 31)

253 Bronze terret (rein-ring), La Tène II
? Paris. D 68mm. M.A.N. 51399. *ECA* no. 175b. (PLATE 31)

254 Bronze head, La Tène II
? Paris. H 29mm. M.A.N. 51402. *ECA* no. 175c. (PLATE 31)

Comparisons: France and Britain

Undoubtedly there are links between British and continental artefacts, but the comparisons are rarely exact. Before Caesar's invasions of Britain continental imports, of objects or craftsmen, are extremely rare. British craftsmen maintained contact with developments abroad, but without loss of a distinctive native flavour. Some part of that contact obviously involved France, and in the following section of the catalogue the opportunity has been taken to set French and British objects side by side. As a contribution to the study of La Tène artefacts this approach is limited and highly selective, but it takes advantage of a unique opportunity to compare and contrast objects found on both sides of the English Channel.

Art

Whilst some comparison may be made between the development of La Tène art in Britain and France, essentially the important works of art from the two countries are chronologically complementary. The major French pieces belong to the earlier part of the La Tène period, whereas the real floruit of British La Tène art came in the couple of centuries before the Roman conquest.

Classical designs can be distinguished on two interesting British pieces. First, the bronze fragments from Cerrig-y-drudion, in Wales, which have been restored into a hanging-bowl – a form unique in the La Tène world (no. 255). The upright and reversed 'palmettes' are linked by fat-stemmed forms to create a continuous border round the rim. The relationship between these motifs and some French pieces (nos 222–228; see Fig. 2) is clear, although Cerrig-y-drudion includes another device, which has been identified as a devolved acanthus leaf. The linking forms on the rim, and similar curved motifs on the body of the bowl, may be compared with the other early British piece, part of a decorated scabbard or sheath from an old collection formed at Wisbech (no. 256). The surviving part of the scabbard-plate has an overall pattern of linked s-forms, or lyre-motifs – a design recalling the openwork 'yoke-mount' from Somme-Tourbe (no. 231).

Waldalgesheim art in Britain is represented by the delicate tendril design in very low relief on a bracelet from Newnham Croft, near Cambridge (no. 257), and the

design on the top of a 'horn-cap' from the Thames at Brentford (no. 258). The Brentford design is basically tripartite: three pelta-like forms, perhaps derived from palmettes, are linked by triangular shapes which give rise to 'bird-headed' tendrils. The huge stone at Turoe (there is a replica of the stone; see no. 259) is shown as a contrast to the small metal objects: its complex design is rooted in Waldalgesheim art, but authorities place it in the first century BC.

255 Bronze fragments restored as a hanging-bowl,
La Tène I
Cerrig-y-drudion (Denbighshire). D 265mm. National Museum of Wales, 26.116. R. A. Smith 'Two early British bronze bowls', *Antiq. Journ.* 6 (1926) 276–83; *PP* I, fig. 1; *ECA* pl. 279, no. 471.

256 Upper part of a bronze scabbard-plate,
La Tène I
Probably found near Wisbech (Cambridgeshire).
L 128mm. Wisbech and Fenland Museum. S. Piggott, 'Swords and Scabbards of the British Early Iron Age', *Proc. Prehist. Soc.* 16 (1950) 1–28, fig. 1; *PP* 1–3, fig. 2. (PLATE 32)

257 Bronze bracelet, La Tène I/II
Newnham Croft (Cambridgeshire) D 78mm. University Museum of Archaeology and Anthropology, Cambridge. C. Fox, *Archaeology of the Cambridge Region* (1923) 81, pl. xv; M. D. Craister, 'Iron Age grave group from Newnham Croft, Cambridge', *Proc. Camb. Ant. Soc.* 64 (1973) 25; *PP* II, fig. 6a.

258 Bronze 'horn-cap', La Tène I/II
River Thames at Brentford, London. H 62mm. The Museum of London, Layton Collection no. 0.1760. R. A. Smith, 'Specimens from the Layton Collection in Brentford Public Library', *Arch.* 69 (1917–18) 1–30, fig. 22; *PP* 3, pls. 3a–c and 4; P-M. Duval, 'L'ornament de char de Brentford (Middlesex)', in P.-M. Duval (ed.), *Recherches d'archéologie celtique et gallo-romaine* Hautes Etudes du monde Greco-Romaine, 5 (1973) 3–10. (PLATE 32)

259 Replica of a decorated granite erratic,
La Tène III
Turoe, County Galway. H 1680mm. B.M. (replica). M. Duignan, 'The Turoe stone: its place in insular La Tène art', in P.-M. Duval & C. F. C. Hawkes (eds.),

The circular shield-boss from the River Thames at Wandsworth (no. 260) has some features – the broad swelling stems and 'bird-heads' – which hint at Waldalgesheim roots, but the engraved ornament is something quite different. Similarly, the design on the upper part of a scabbard from the River Witham (no. 261) is executed in both repoussé and engraving. The engraving on these pieces has some link with continental 'Sword Style' ornament, a style hardly represented in France and not shown in the present exhibition because the famous Cernon-sur-Coole scabbard was unfortunately too fragile to travel. From this point insular La Tène art flourishes independently of continental influence. The high relief plastic ornament in France has no counterpart in Britain, where the ornament is more linear, usually engraved and chased, and even where ornament was cast it was in low relief. This is not the place to trace its further development and glorify its achievement, but some suggestion of its quality is given by three relatively new acquisitions to the British Museum collection (nos 262-264).

260 Bronze shield-boss, La Tène II
River Thames at Wandsworth, London. D 330mm.
B.M. 58.11–16.2. J. M. Kemble, *Horae Ferales* (1863)
191, pl. xvi, no. 1; *PP* 25–6, pl. 13.

261 Iron sword with the upper part of a bronze scabbard-plate, La Tène II
River Witham, below Lincoln. L 630mm. Alnwick Castle Museum, no. 276. P. Jacobsthal, 'The Witham sword', *The Burlington Magazine* 75 (1939) 28–31;
PP 25, pl. 22b. (PLATE 32)

262 Bronze scabbard-plate, La Tène II
River Bann (County Londonderry). L 420mm. B.M. (deposited on loan by W. M. Jackson Esq. in 1979).
J. Raftery, *Prehistoric Ireland* (1951) fig. 216. (PLATE 32)

263 Bronze mirror, La Tène III
Aston (Hertfordshire). D 194mm. B.M. P.1979.10–2.1.
Unpublished. (PLATE 33)

264 Bronze scabbard, La Tène III
Isleham (Cambridgeshire). L 767mm. B.M. P.1976.7–3.1.
Unpublished. (PLATE 34)

Dagger-sheaths

A series of dagger-sheaths dating from the fifth century BC provides one of the most interesting comparisons between British and French La Tène antiquities. The sheaths are made from two metal plates, with the edges of the bronze front-plate wrapped round to clasp the iron back-plate, and a separate bronze chape securing the two at the bottom. The French specimens were found in graves in Champagne, whereas the British pieces were dredged out of the River Thames. The development of the chape is closely matched on both sides of the Channel – it starts as a socket with anchor-like terminal (no. 265), the arms of the 'anchor' curve back to the chape (no. 266), and eventually form a framework which replaces the socket (nos 267–272). There was obviously a very close contact between the two areas, but one detail emphasises that they were not exchanged: the British sheaths regularly have a suspension-loop formed of two separate bands (no. 272) but the French examples always have a single band (no. 271; see Fig. 6).

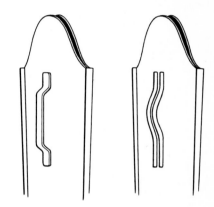

Fig. 6 *Suspension-loops of French* (left) *and British dagger-sheaths.*

265 Bronze front of a sheath, La Tène I
River Thames at Chelsea, London. L 322mm.
B.M. 98.6–18.1. E. M. Jope, 'Daggers of the Early Iron Age in Britain', *Proc. Prehist. Soc.* 27 (1961) 307–43, no. 11.

266 Bronze and iron sheath, La Tène I
River Thames at Barn Elms, London. L 295mm.
B.M. WG.2356. Jope, *op. cit.*, no. 13.

267 Bronze and iron sheath, La Tène I
St Jean-sur-Tourbe (Marne). L 263mm. M.A.N. 20266.
Champagne pl. 84, fig. 5. (PLATE 34)

268 Iron dagger in bronze and iron sheath,
La Tène I
Provenance unknown (Champagne). L 355mm.
B.M. ML.2401.

269 Iron dagger in a bronze and iron sheath,
La Tène I
River Thames at Hammersmith, London. L 330mm.
B.M. 1906.5–30.1. Jope, *op. cit.*, no. 18.

270 Iron dagger in a bronze and iron sheath,
La Tène I
River Thames at Battersea, London. L 284mm.
B.M. 59.1–22.8. Jope, *op. cit.*, no. 17.

271 Bent iron dagger in an iron sheath, La Tène I
Provenance unknown (Champagne). Shows the typical
French suspension loop. L (when straight) 270mm.
B.M. ML.2601.

272 Iron dagger in a bronze and iron sheath,
La Tène I
River Thames at Wandsworth, London. Shows the
typical British suspension loop. L 312mm.
B.M. 53.3–24.1. Jope, *op. cit.*, no. 22; *PP* pl. 10a;
Manuel fig. 457, no. 6.

Swords

Later British swords are quite distinct from their French
counterparts, one obvious difference being the British
preference for bronze scabbards whereas iron was used in
France. However, one type of French weapon, a form of
short sword which sometimes accompanies the more
typical long slashing sword, has striking parallels in
Britain. These short swords have iron blades but hilts of
bronze, and the finest examples have well-modelled
heads on the pommels (nos 273–276).

273 Iron sword with bronze hilt, La Tène II
Salon (Aube). L 460mm. B.M. ML.1669. R. R. Clarke
& C. F. C. Hawkes, 'An iron anthropoid sword from
Shouldham, Norfolk, with related continental and
British weapons', *Proc. Prehist. Soc.* 21 (1955) 198–227,
no. 35; *CS* pl. 33, fig. 1; *Manuel* fig. 474, no. 1.

274 Iron sword with bronze hilt, La Tène II
Châtenay-Mâcheron (Haute-Marne). L 425mm.
M.A.N. 28216. Clarke & Hawkes, *op. cit.*, no. 27;
Manuel fig. 474. no. 3. (PLATE 34)

275 Iron sword with bronze hilt, La Tène II
North Grimston (North Yorkshire). L 509mm. Hull
Museums and Art Galleries. Clarke & Hawkes, *op. cit.*,
no. 44; *Arras*, 61, figs. 21, no. 1 and 22, no. 1; *PP* 30,
pl. 18. (PLATE 34)

276 Iron sword with bronze hilt, La Tène III
Provenance unknown, possibly Yorkshire. L 466mm.
B.M. 88.7–19.36. Clarke & Hawkes. *op. cit.*, no. 49.

Shields

Celtic shields in Britain and France seem to have been
quite similar in shape, although there are marked differences in the metal fittings. As with the sword-scabbards,
iron was the prefered metal on the Continent, whereas
bronze was used in Britain. But there is not much

comparison between the metal fittings, for the normal
continental band-shaped umbo (no. 98) has no counterpart. In Britain the metal tended to cover the length
instead of the width of the central boss, and sometimes the
full length of the central spine was encased. A couple of
shields from Champagne also had the central spine
covered in bronze, and one has an approach to the band-
shaped umbo as well (no. 277). The body of the British
shield was occasionally decorated with pieces of sheet
bronze (no. 278) and, indeed, there are British shields
covered entirely with bronze. Other shields, throughout
the Celtic provinces, seem to have had plaques or discs
of metal as ornament or devices readily recognisable in
battle (nos 279–281).

277 Bronze fittings of a shield, La Tène II
Vicinity of the Camp de Châlons (Marne). L 547mm.
M.A.N. 18742. *Dictionnaire Archéologique de la Gaule*,
i (1875) unnumbered pl., fig. 2; *Manuel* 1172, note 3;
G. Ritchie, *Celtic defensive weaponry in Britain and its
continental background* (1969) unpublished Ph.D. thesis,
111 and pl. 23.

278 Bronze fittings of a shield, La Tène III
Grimthorpe (North Humberside). L (large plaques)
312mm. B.M. 72.2–8.1, 2, 5–8. *Arras* 55–7; *PP* 35,
pl. 23c.

279 Bronze disc, La Tène III
Grimthorpe (North Humberside). Possibly from a
shield. D 48mm. B.M. 76.2–8.3. *Arras* 57–8; *PP* 35,
pl. 23b.

280 Bronze discs with red glass ornaments,
La Tène III
Bugthorpe (North Humberside). Possibly from a
shield. D 58, 49mm. B.M. 1905.7–17.4 and 5. *Arras*
58–9; *PP* pl. 11c. (PLATE 35)

281 Iron and coral disc, La Tène I/II
Vicinity of the Camp de Châlons (Marne). Possibly
from a shield. D 57mm. M.A.N. 13672. *ECA* no. 345;
V. Moucha, 'Latènezeitliche Gräber aus Sulejovice in
Nordwestböhmen', *Arch. Rozhledy* 21 (1969) 596–617,
fig. 6. (PLATE 35)

Glass beads

In Britian the burials most nearly comparable to those in
Champagne are found on the Yorkshire Wolds – but
there are many differences between the rites in the two
areas. In Yorkshire crouched skeletons were placed in
graves under barrows, whilst in Champagne extended
skeletons in flat-graves were the rule. Weapons are rare
and jewellery is usually simpler and locally made.
Torques are unknown in Yorkshire, but there are
occasional necklaces of glass beads which offer some

close comparisons with the few bead necklaces from Champagne (nos 282–285). In particular, the blue beads are very similar: plain blue; blue with a zig-zag white trail; and blue with 'eyes' formed by white inserts with added blue centres.

282 Twenty-three glass beads, La Tène I
Bussy-le-Château (Marne). D (largest bead) 12mm.
M.A.N. 13195. (PLATE 35)

283 Thirty-eight glass and five amber beads,
La Tène I
Bergères-lès-Vertus (Marne). D (largest bead) 35mm.
M.A.N. 12012. Excavated by Charles Leboeuf, cf.
CS 103–5.

284 Fifty-four glass beads, La Tène I/II
Queen's Barrow, Arras (North Humberside). D 11–
18mm. Yorkshire Museum, York. Arras 78–80.

285 Sixty-seven glass beads, La Tène I/II
Wetwang Slack (North Humberside). D 10–12mm.
J. S. Dent excavations. Unpublished; for the site see
J. S. Dent, 'Wetwang Slack', Current Arch. 61 (1978)
46–50.

Coral

Precious coral (Coralium rubrum) was used for decoration, and 'the Gauls were in the habit of adorning their swords, shields, and helmets with it' (Pliny, Nat. Hist., 32. 11). There were important coral fisheries round the shores of the western Mediterranean, and Pliny also recorded that 'the most highly-esteemed of all is that produced in the vicinity of the islands called Stoechades, in the Gallic Gulf' (the Hyères Islands, off the coast of Provence). Branches of coral were sometimes used for pendants (no. 287) and short lengths were strung as beads (no. 288), whilst pieces of all sizes were used on a wider range of objects than listed by Pliny – especially on brooches (nos 294–297). Only rarely does the rich pink colour survive, for coral found in archaeological contexts is usually now white. One of the curiosities concerning coral-ornament in ancient times is that its main use abroad seems to end before it became popular in Britain. Coral was used in Britain especially in La Tène II, and provides one of the very rare examples of undoubted trade from the Continent.

286 Piece of precious coral, *Corallium rubrum*
H 200mm. British Museum (Natural History),
Department of Zoology.

287 Coral branches wrapped with bronze and strung with an amber bead for use as a pendant,
La Tène I
Somme-Bionne (Marne). L 29mm. B.M. ML.1419.
CS pl. 13, fig. 12; Manuel fig. 560, no. 5.

288 Coral necklace, La Tène I
Provenance unknown (Champagne). L 6–19mm.
B.M. ML.2240.

289 Coral necklace, La Tène I
Camp de Châlons (Marne). Composed of pieces from 5–22mm. long, with one amber bead (D 11mm).
M.A.N. 15996.

290 Bronze nail-cleaner with coral beads,
La Tène I
Ecury-sur-Coole (Marne). L 81mm. M.A.N. 77050.
Grave 11. A. Thiérot, 'Fond de cabane de l'époque hallstattienne, cimetières celtiques, tombe gallo-romaine des "Côtes-en-Marne" à Ecury-sur-Coole', Bull. Soc. Arch. Champenoise (1931) 36–56, fig. p. 53; Champagne pl. 132, no. 10. (PLATE 35)

291 Bronze torque with beads of coral and glass,
La Tène I
La Cheppe (Marne). D 142mm. M.A.N. 23039.

292 Bronze bracelet with beads of coral,
La Tène II
Burton Fleming (North Humberside). D 60mm.
B.M. P.1978.12–2. Arras 73, fig. 29, no. 2.

293 Bronze brooch, La Tène I
Mauvilly (Côte-d'Or). With a central amber bead ringed by small coral beads. D 35mm. M.A.N. 427.
R. Joffroy, 'Le mobilier du Tumulus de la Friche à Mauvilly (Côte-d'Or)', Rev. Arch. de l'Est et du Centre-Est, 11 (1960) 204–14, fig. 77, no. 4. (PLATE 36)

294 Bronze brooch with coral ornament,
La Tène I
Pleurs (Marne). L 73mm. B.M. ML.1631. CS pl. 27, fig. 3. (PLATE 36)

295 Bronze brooch with coral ornament,
La Tène II?
Pleurs (Marne). L 82mm. B.M. ML.1632. This unusual brooch may be compared with one from St Benôit-sur-Seine (Aube), a cemetery which seems to be mainly La Tène II, Gallia 25 (1967) 277–9, fig. 14; CS pl. 29, fig. 4. (PLATE 36)

296 Bronze brooch with coral ornament,
La Tène I/II
Queen's Barrow, Arras (North Humberside). L 66mm.
Yorkshire Museum, York. Arras 66, fig. 23, no. 3;
PP pl. 9c and d. (PLATE 36)

297 Bronze brooch with coral ornament and iron pin, La Tène I
Wetwang Slack (North Humberside). L 63mm.
J. S. Dent excavations. Unpublished (see no. 285).
(PLATE 36)

Pottery

One of the most satisfying decorative styles found on British pottery of any period is 'Glastonbury Ware', named after the Iron Age lake village where it was excavated in quantity between 1892 and 1907. On a range of glossy black and dark grey vessels intricate curvilinear scrolls and geometric designs were outlined with a fine incised line and infilled and highlighted with hatching. There were a number of different production centres, and the wares were traded to settlements in south-western Britain.

Stylistically and technically Glastonbury Wares appear to be closely related to decorated vessels found in Armorica. A comparison of the fine Breton jar (no. 298), which was found in a cremation burial dated to the fourth century BC, with the jar from the settlement at Meare (no. 299; see Fig. 7), well illustrates this.

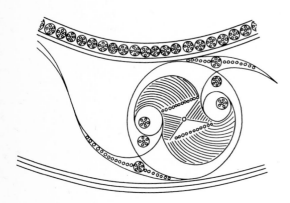

Fig. 7 *The design on a pot from Meare, no. 299 (after Bulleid & Gray).*

The upper section of the handmade shouldered jar from Margate (no. 304) shows how the running-scroll motif was adapted by a potter working somewhere in south-eastern Britain in the second and early first centuries BC. The design was outlined by broad grooves, instead of the fine incised lines used on Glastonbury Ware, and the filling was roughened and then textured with 'pecking' in contrast to the glossy surface of the rest of the pot. The effect is much freer than that achieved by the Glastonbury potters. Only two comparable pots have been recognised, at Mucking, Thurrock (Essex), and Newhaven (Sussex), coastal locations which suggest distribution by sea.

298 Shouldered jar, La Tène I
Kélouer, Plouhinec (Finistère). Handmade. H 310mm. M.A.N. 72933. Abbé Abgrall, 'Station gaulois de Broën et Trez-Neven, à Plouhinec (Finistère)', *Matériaux pour l'histoire primitive et naturelle de l'homme* (1882–3) 520; *Manuel* fig. 663, no. 2.

299 Shouldered jar, La Tène II/III
Meare Lake Village (Somerset). Handmade. H 355mm. Somerset County Museum, Taunton, P. 249. A. Bulleid & H. St G. Gray, *The Meare Lake Village* I (1948) fig. 4.

300 Lid, La Tène II/III
Glastonbury Lake Village (Somerset). Handmade. D 170mm. Somerset County Museum, Taunton, 159.

301 Bowl, La Tène II/III
Meare Lake Village (Somerset). Handmade. D 264mm. Somerset County Museum, Taunton, P. 113. Bulleid & Gray, *op. cit.* 37, pl. VIII & XVI.

302 Shouldered bowl, La Tène II/III
Meare Lake Village (Somerset). Handmade. H 135mm. Somerset County Museum, Taunton, P. 19. Bulleid & Gray, *op. cit.,* pl. XV.

303 Shouldered bowl, La Tène II/III
Meare Lake Village (Somerset). Handmade. H 120mm. Somerset County Museum, Taunton, P. 27. Bulleid & Gray *op. cit.* pl. V & XIX.

304 Shouldered jar, La Tène II/III
Margate (Kent). Handmade. H 120mm (as found). B.M. 1926.10–19.1. *Antiq. Journ.* 5 (1925) 164–5.

Gold torques

Torques found in graves in Champagne are usually made of bronze, rarely of iron, but never of gold; they are always found in the graves of women and not in the graves of men. Yet representations show warriors and gods adorned with neck-rings, and there can be no doubt that the Gauls wore gold torques in battle. Describing the Battle of Telamon, Polybius (II.29) records that 'all the warriors in the front ranks were adorned in gold necklaces and bracelets', and Diodorus Siculus (V.27.3) mentions 'round their necks thick rings of solid gold'. Several explanations have been offered for the absence of torques from warriors' graves in Champagne: the Gauls mentioned in the literary sources were in Italy and could have had different traditions from those whose graves have been explored in northern France; there could be a chronological disparity, for the torques in graves are essentially from the fifth and fourth centuries, whereas the historical accounts are of the third century and later; gold torques might perhaps have been placed in graves, and subsequently robbed; or gold torques could have been worn by men but never assigned to the graves. Beyond Champagne gold torques are occasionally found in graves, but most were chance finds, either isolated or in hoards.

The fine gold torque from Mailly (no. 307) was found by chance in 1965. It is tubular and seems to have been filled with wax round an iron core. The Mailly torque is particularly interesting because there is a suggestion that it belonged to a ritual hoard. On the inner face there are six inscriptions in Greek characters, and it has been argued that one refers to its dedication whilst others record additions to a treasure – it was both an offering and a register of further offerings. Diodorus Siculus (v.27) gives a possible context: 'a large amount of gold is openly placed as a dedication to the gods, and of the native inhabitants none touch it because of religious veneration, although the Celts are unusually fond of money'. Although the Mailly torque was found in Champagne, the inscriptions on it mention the tribe of Nitiobroges who lived in south-western France.

One of the closest parallels for the Mailly torque was found only seventeen years previously as a result of the first deep-ploughing of a field at Snettisham, in Norfolk. In the course of two ploughings five groups of metalwork and coins were revealed, including many gold objects. It has been suggested that the Snettisham hoards were the stock-in-trade of a metalsmith, which for greater security was divided into groups when it was concealed. The large tubular torque from hoard 'A' (no. 308) is very similar to that from Mailly, and it too has a filling of wax, and sand, round an iron core. Another torque from the Snettisham collection, from hoard 'D' (no. 309) is of a very different form, with two gold strands twisted together and looped at the terminals.

305 Gold torque, La Tène I
'Found in France'. D 140mm. B.M. 67.5–8.477.
ECA no. 39.

306 Gold torque, La Tène I/II
Provenance unknown. D 152mm. B.M. S. Birch, 'On the torc of the Celts', *Arch. Journ.* 3 (1846) 27–38, fig. p. 31; *ECA* no. 40 (Jacobsthal considered that the knot has 'superstitious significance').

307 Gold torque, La Tène III
Mailly-le-Camp (Aube). D 198mm. M.A.N. 82988. R. Joffroy, 'Le torque de Mailly-le-Camp', *Monuments et mémoires* 56 (1969) 45–59; and an account of the inscriptions, M. Lejeune, 'Les graffites gallo-grecs du torque de Mailly-le-Camp', *ibid.*, 61–76. (PLATE 37)

308 Gold torque, La Tène III
Snettisham (Norfolk). D 230mm. Castle Museum, Norwich. R. R. Clarke, 'The Early Iron Age treasure from Snettisham, Norfolk', *Proc. Prehist. Soc.* 20 (1954) 27–86, pl. i, no. 1. (PLATE 37)

309 Gold torque, La Tène III
Snettisham (Norfolk). D 212mm. B.M. 1951.4–2.1. Clarke, *op. cit.*, pl. x.

The Supernatural

Most of the objects in this catalogue come from burials, and it must be obvious that the Gauls respected their dead and envisaged some kind of existence after death. The dead were accompanied by their everyday possessions and provided with food and drink which implies sustenance for a journey if not for a life hereafter. But artefacts tell us very little about beliefs and the absence of a Celtic literature leaves the field of the supernatural wide open to speculation. Caesar (*De Bello Gallico* VI.19.4) refers to Gallic burial practices (in his day cremation was the rule): 'Funerals are on a large and expensive scale, considering the Gallic way of life; everything which they believe the dead man loved in life is given to the flames, even the animals; and it is only a short time since the slaves and clients who were known to have been loved by the dead man were cremated along with him when the funeral was properly carried out'. Diodorus Siculus (V.28.6) comments that the Gauls believe 'that the souls of men are immortal, and that after a definite number of years they live a second life when the soul passes into another body. This is the reason given why some people at the burial of the dead cast upon the pyre letters written to their dead relatives, thinking that the dead will be able to read them'. But by and large writers of an alien culture are a poor source for religious beliefs.

In all probability Celtic gods were of purely local significance, and Roman attempts to correlate them with their own deities imposed a uniformity quite foreign to Celtic religion. Only rarely were Gallic gods represented in materials more durable than wood, and the most famous of the survivors are illustrated here. The magnificent bronze figure from Bouray (no. 310), depicting a god wearing a torque, was dredged from the River Juine some forty kilometres south of Paris in 1845. The cross-legged squatting posture is known from other representations of gods, and is the natural position for people who had no need of stools or chairs, but 'sit on dried grass and have their meals served up on wooden tables raised slightly above the earth' (Athenaeus IV. 36). Authorities are undecided about the date of the Bouray god, and a similar problem is presented by the finely carved limestone figure found at Euffigneix (no. 311). Only the head and trunk survive, and the head has been mutilated, but the Euffigneix god also wears a torque and

sports a fine representation of a boar – a favourite Celtic animal which is still used as the symbol of the Ardennes Département.

The double-headed 'Janus' god in reddish limestone, with bald heads, large oval eyes and narrow twisted mouths (no. 312) comes from the hinterland of Marseille, a fringe area of Gallic culture tainted with Greek and Roman influence. A Greek settlement was founded at Marseille about 600 BC, and colonists introduced their own customs and practices, including houses and temples built of stone. In the surrounding countryside there emerged a distinctive native culture, whose constructions in stone stood a far better chance of survival than the wooden buildings used by the Gauls further north. Some of the statuary from the south of France has already been mentioned earlier in the catalogue (nos 93 and 94). The 'Janus' god and a frieze of horse heads (no. 313) come from Roquepertuse, near Aix-en-Provence, where there was a sanctuary whose stone portico is now re-built in the Musée Borély at Marseille. The pillars of the portico have niches – three in the centre and one at each side – each originally the seat for a human skull.

But stone sanctuaries were not normally used by the Gauls, although we know very little about such matters. Lucan, a Roman poet writing in the first century AD about events which took place a century earlier, refers to a sacred wood desecrated by Caesar (*Pharsalia* III. 399–423): 'A grove there was, untouched by men's hands from ancient times, whose interlacing boughs enclosed a space of darkness and cold shade, and banished the sunlight from above . . . gods were worshipped there with savage rites, the altars were heaped with hideous offerings, and every tree was sprinkled with human gore . . . The images of the gods, grim and rude, were uncouth blocks, formed of felled tree-trunks . . . The people never resorted thither to worship at close quarters, but left the place to the gods'. Such sacred places and wooden images would leave little trace for the archaeologist unless exceptional conditions aided their preservation. Elsewhere Lucan mentions the druids, whose barbarous ceremonials were carried out in deep glades within remote forests. These druids were perhaps philosophers and teachers rather than priests, whose activities were deliberately shrouded in secrecy, and who relied entirely on speech instead of writing for conveying their beliefs and traditions. Their rejection of literature is of course one of the main reasons why we know so little about the Gauls.

310 Bronze figure of a god with an eye of glass,
La Tène III
Bouray-sur-Juine (Essone). H 420mm. M.A.N. 76551.
R. Lantier, 'Le dieu celtique de Bouray', *Monuments et mémoires* 34 (1934) 35–58. (PLATE 38)

311 Limestone figure of a god, La Tène III
Euffigneix (Haute-Marne). H 300mm. M.A.N. 78243.
E. Esperandieu, '*Recueil général des bas-reliefs, statues et bustes de la Gaule romaine* xi (1938) no. 7702.
(PLATE 39)

312 Replica of a limestone sculpture of two heads,
La Tène II
Roquepertuse (Bouches-du-Rhône). H 195mm.
Musée Borély, Marseille. E. Esperandieu, *op. cit.,* x (1928) no. 7616; F. Benoit, *L'art primitif mediterranéen de la vallée du Rhône* (1955) pl. xxxiv, no. 1, and pl. xxv. (PLATE 37)

313 Limestone block carved with horse heads,
La Tène II
Roquepertuse (Bouches-du-Rhône). L 600mm. Musée Borély, Marseille. F. Beniot, *op. cit.,* pl. xiii. (PLATE 39)

Some outstanding antiquities and fascinating glimpses of Gallic life, and death, have been provided by chance finds and the work of nineteenth-century collectors. Classical writers record some history and ethnography, but the absence of a native literature means that a vast area of Gallic culture will for every remain unknown. Nonetheless, there is more information to be recovered about domestic sites, agriculture, technology and many other aspects of society. The present generation of French archaeologists is working hard towards these ends, and every year we learn a little more about the Gauls.

PLATE 1

Napoléon III

Frédéric Moreau

Léon Morel

Marquis de Baye

PLATE 2

30

67   61   46

PLATE 3

Reconstruction of the Somme-Bionne cart-burial

PLATE 4

79

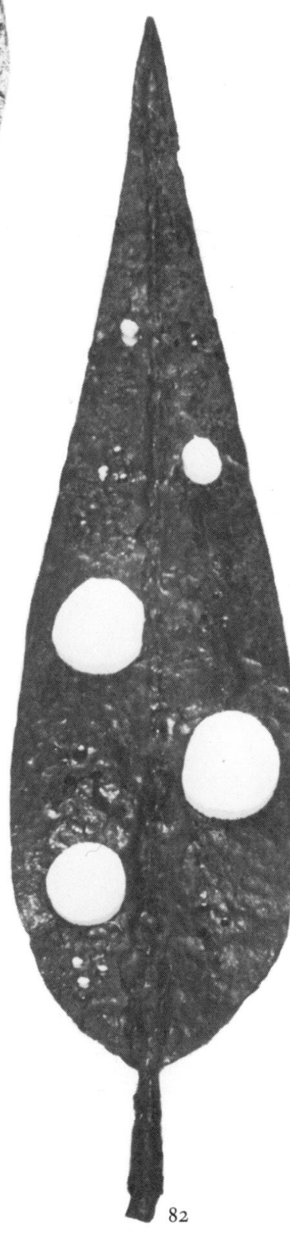

82

PLATE 5

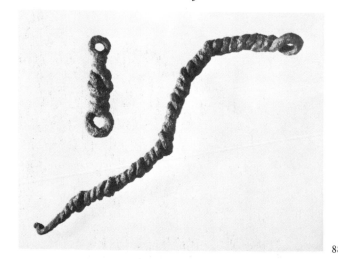

86

88

89

PLATE 6

91

92

90

PLATE 7

93

PLATE 8

PLATE 9

98

102

101

PLATE 10

106

111

PLATE 11

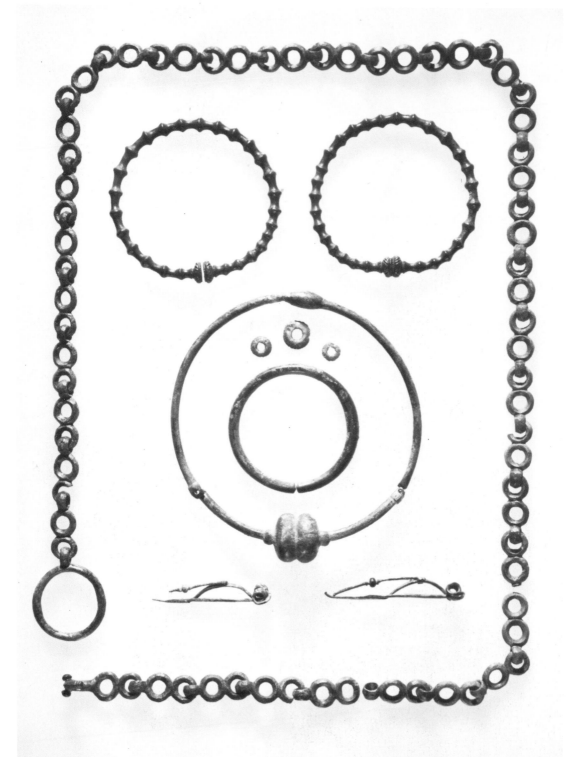

PLATE 12

119

113

129

PLATE 13

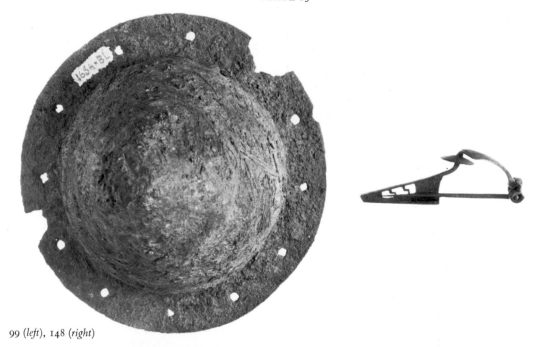

99 (*left*), 148 (*right*)

PLATE 14

159

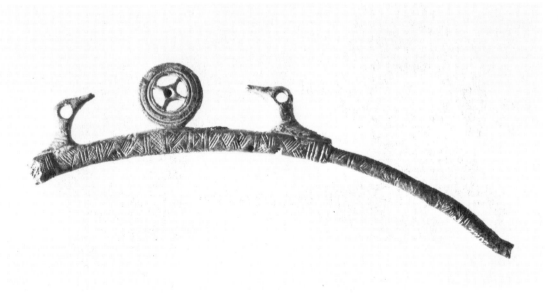

162

PLATE 15

Left to right 167, 39, 166, 38

Back 173 (*left*), 174 (*right*); *front* 172 (*left*), 171 (*centre*), 169 (*right*)

PLATE 16

176

183

184 (*left*), 182 (*centre*), 181 (*right*)

PLATE 17

43 (*left*), 44 (*centre*), 185 (*right*)

186

PLATE 18

192 (*left*), 193 (*right*)

194

196

PLATE 19

198

202

200

PLATE 20

PLATE 21

PLATE 22

222

223

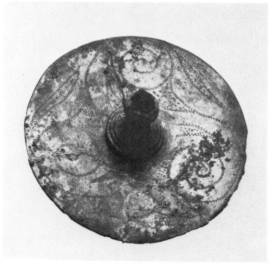

225

227

PLATE 23

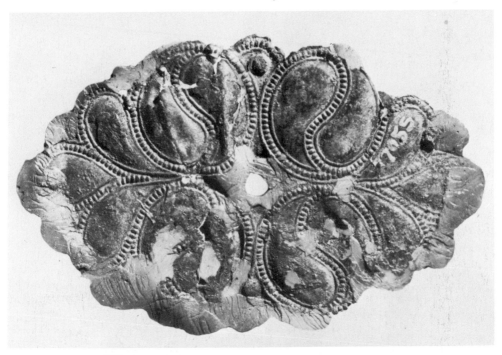

230

228

PLATE 24

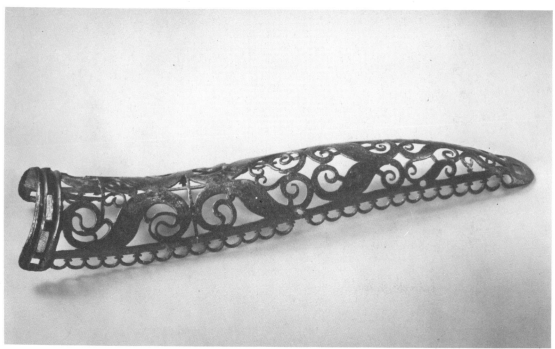

231

232

PLATE 25

233

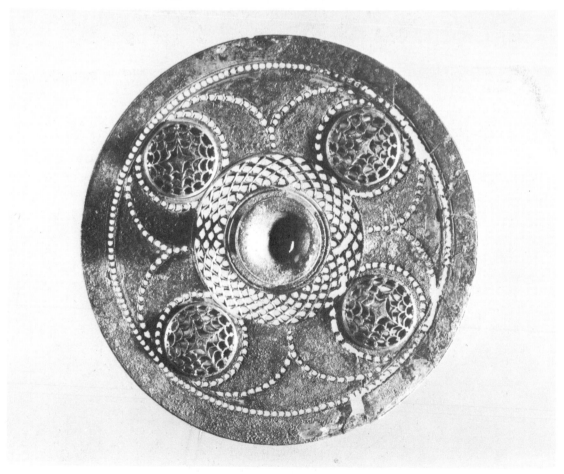

235

PLATE 26

236

Drawing of the design on 236

PLATE 27

237

238

PLATE 28

239

240

PLATE 29

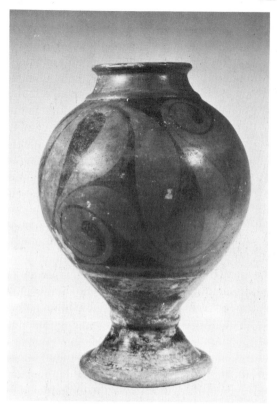

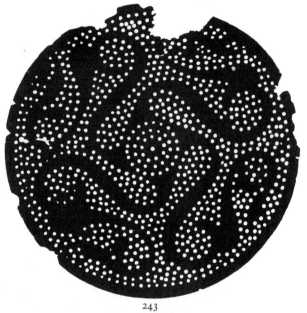

241

243

134 (*left*), 246 (*centre*), 138 (*right*)

PLATE 30

249

250

251

PLATE 31

252

253

254

PLATE 32

258

256

259

Drawing of 262   261

PLATE 33

PLATE 34

267

264

274

275

PLATE 35

280

281

290

282

PLATE 36

293

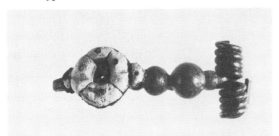

294

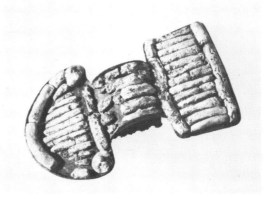

295

296

297

PLATE 37

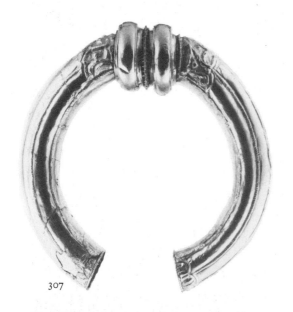

307

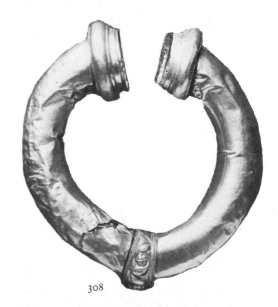

308

312

PLATE 38

PLATE 39

311, *with side view (right)*   186

313